Other books by Eric Sloane available as Dover reprints

A Museum of Early American Tools
American Barns and Covered Bridges
American Yesterday
A Reverence for Wood
Look at the Sky and Tell the Weather
Our Vanishing Landscape
Diary of an Early American Boy: Noah Blake 1805
The Seasons of America Past
The Cracker Barrel
Once Upon a Time: The Way America Was
Eric Sloane's Weather Book
Recollections in Black and White
Return to Taos: Eric Sloane's Sketchbook of Roadside Americana

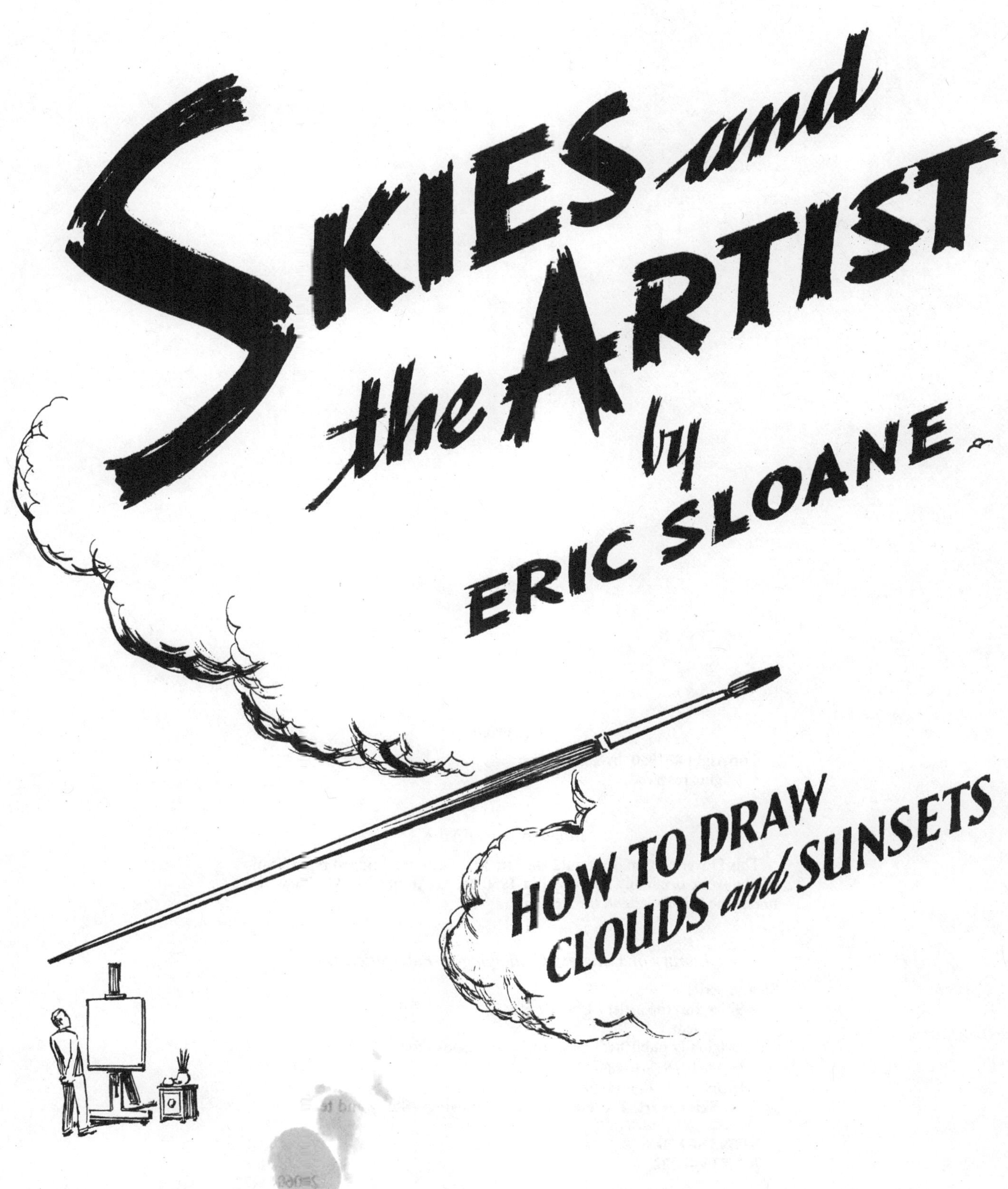

DOVER PUBLICATIONS, INC., MINEOLA, NEW YORK

Bibliographical Note

This Dover edition, first published in 2006, is an unabridged republication of the work originally published in 1950 by Art Books for All, New York, under the title *Skies and the Artist.*

Library of Congress Cataloging-in-Publication Data

Sloane, Eric.
Skies and the artist / Eric Sloane.
p. cm.
Originally published: New York : Art Books for All, 1950.
ISBN-13: 978-0-486-45102-2 (pbk.)
ISBN-10: 0-486-45102-X (pbk.)
1. Skies in art. 2. Clouds in art. 3. Drawing—Study and teaching.

NC795.S49 2006
743'.836—dc22

2006045425

Printed in Canada
45102X08 2025
www.doverpublications.com

SKIES and the ARTIST

HOW TO DRAW CLOUDS and SUNSETS

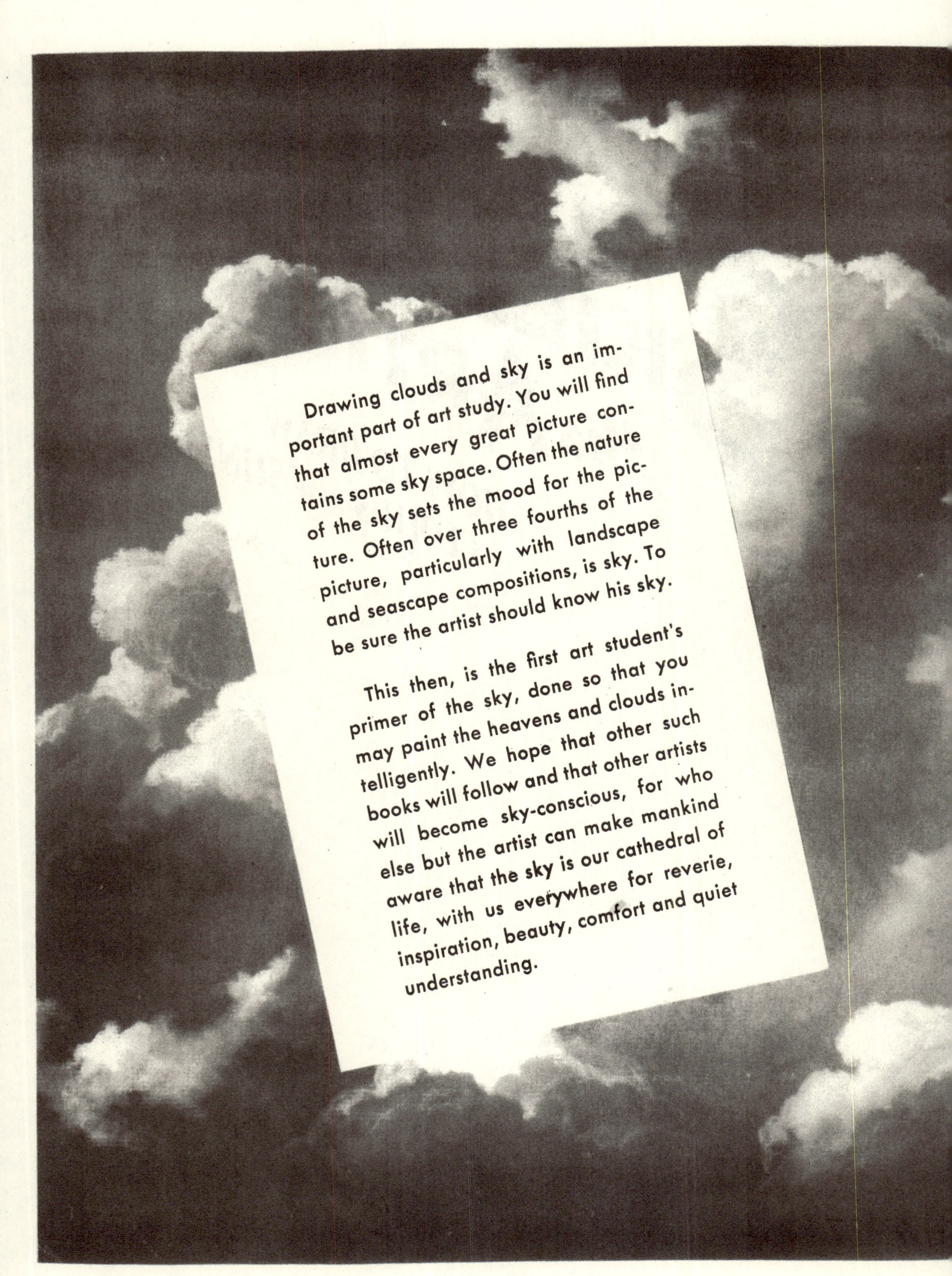
Drawing clouds and sky is an important part of art study. You will find that almost every great picture contains some sky space. Often the nature of the sky sets the mood for the picture. Often over three fourths of the picture, particularly with landscape and seascape compositions, is sky. To be sure the artist should know his sky.
This then, is the first art student's primer of the sky, done so that you may paint the heavens and clouds intelligently. We hope that other such books will follow and that other artists will become sky-conscious, for who else but the artist can make mankind aware that the sky is our cathedral of life, with us everywhere for reverie, inspiration, beauty, comfort and quiet understanding.

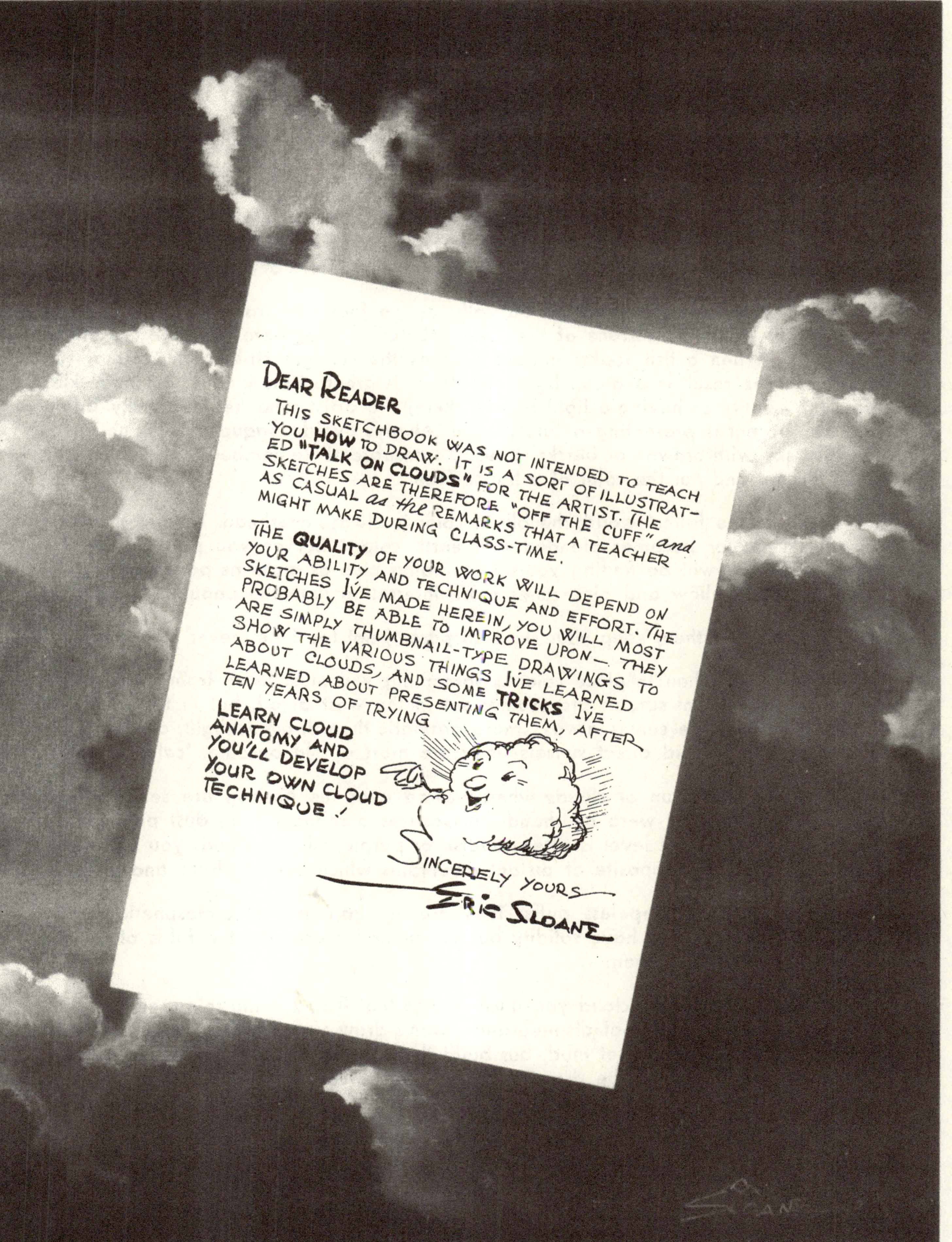

DEAR READER

THIS SKETCHBOOK WAS NOT INTENDED TO TEACH YOU **HOW** TO DRAW. IT IS A SORT OF ILLUSTRATED **"TALK ON CLOUDS"** FOR THE ARTIST. THE SKETCHES ARE THEREFORE "OFF THE CUFF" *and* AS CASUAL *as the* REMARKS THAT A TEACHER MIGHT MAKE DURING CLASS-TIME.

THE **QUALITY** OF YOUR WORK WILL DEPEND ON YOUR ABILITY AND TECHNIQUE AND EFFORT. THE SKETCHES I'VE MADE HEREIN, YOU WILL MOST PROBABLY BE ABLE TO IMPROVE UPON— THEY ARE SIMPLY THUMBNAIL-TYPE DRAWINGS TO SHOW THE VARIOUS THINGS I'VE LEARNED ABOUT CLOUDS, AND SOME **TRICKS** I'VE LEARNED ABOUT PRESENTING THEM, AFTER TEN YEARS OF TRYING.

LEARN CLOUD ANATOMY AND YOU'LL DEVELOP YOUR OWN CLOUD TECHNIQUE!

SINCERELY YOURS

ERIC SLOANE

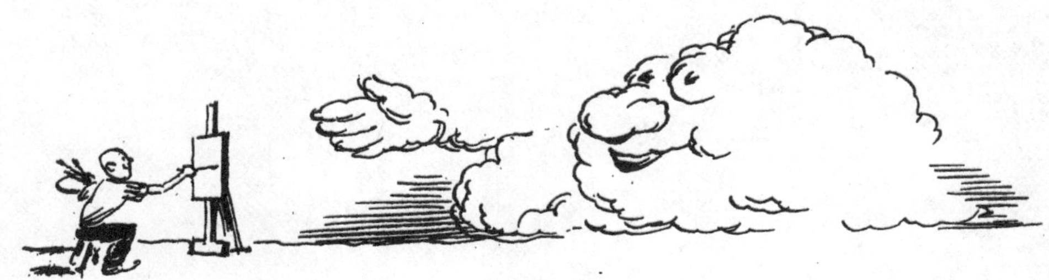

Before talking about drawing the sky and its clouds, it might be well to discuss its anatomy. We shall not delve deeply into meteorology, simply learn the names of things we shall later talk about, and learn about the nature of the atmosphere.

The sky is known to be blue. Actually as we look upward, we are looking at the sunlight strike the surface of the "sea" of stuff (atmosphere) that we are at the bottom of. When a fish looks upward he sees the sunlight striking the top of HIS world and the result is a green light. His "sky" is green. Ours is blue. But both skies have the quality of having a light behind them; the artist who keeps his sky bright and transparent is presenting a true picture. Always avoid opaqueness. Do not muddy your sky with browns or blacks. Keep it transparent! Remember that a blue sky is an illusion and not the color of a flat surface.

Just like the fishes' world, the bluest color is always overhead. Toward the horizon the sky color becomes blended with earth colors. But as you paint more and better skies you will be finding yourself avoiding blue as much as possible; you will find gray and yellow and pink tones more interesting than the popular "sky blue".

Summarizing then, keep your sky transparent, not too blue, never muddy.

Where and when to place color is something you must learn from observation. The most magnificent sunsets are usually not in the west at all, but in the east. The reflected light of the sun is always more dramatic than direct sunlight, and infinitely easier to paint. Avoid direct sunsets: they are most apt to become "calendarish".

The moon, the sun or clouds when viewed over the horizon are seen through more air than if they were overhead. This causes a redness from dust particles, so that the sky at horizon level is often reddish or purple. Distant clouds you will learn, have red tones, the opposite of distant mountains which become hazy and blue.

Clouds are not shapeless puffs. They are the garments of atmospheric waves. Therefore they must not have solidity but action and grace like the folds of a robe worn by someone in action.

To put grace into a cloud you must realize that it is a living thing, either in the process of building up or of disintegration. Don't draw your clouds solidly as if they were sodden mounds of wet mud, but build them up into gaseous billows. They are really wet air in action. The drawing shows how clouds are formed by graceful air currents. It also shows how cloud grace can enter into the action of your picture by "pushing" a boat or "blowing" leaning trees.

It may be difficult to think of clouds as being anything but static lumps. To explain their living action, turn to the next pages to see how a simple fair weather cloud is born.

ALTHOUGH CLOUDS APPEAR MOTIONLESS, THEY *are* REALLY SLOW EXPLOSIONS. WHETHER SINGLE (CUMULUS PUFFS) OR SOLID FLAT LAYERS (STRATOFORM) THEY PUFF *and* BOIL CONTINUALLY.

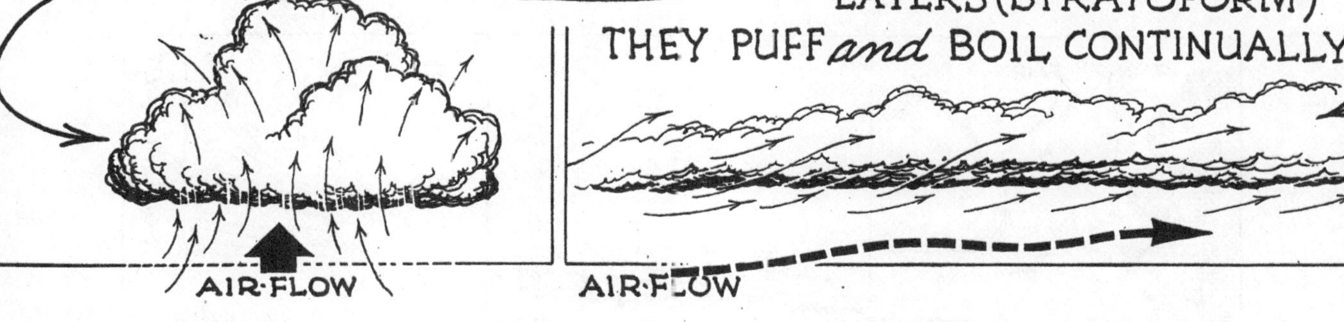

.....THEREFORE DON'T MAKE CLOUD-MASSES LOOK LIKE MELTING MOUNDS OF ICE CREAM BUT LIKE LIVING SHAPES *in* GRACEFUL ACTION

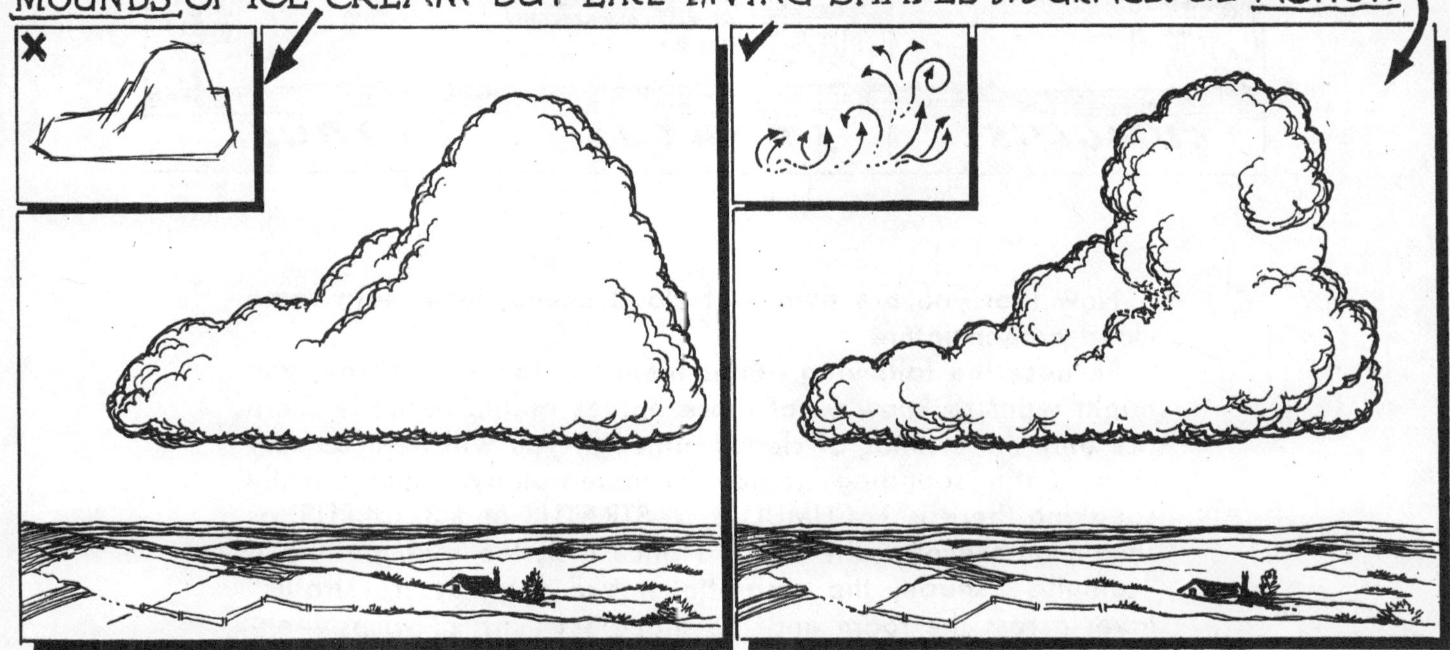

DO THINK OF CLOUD ACTION FIRST, THEN THINK OF CLOUD SHAPE *and* OUTLINE, BECAUSE SHAPE DEPENDS *upon* MOVEMENT

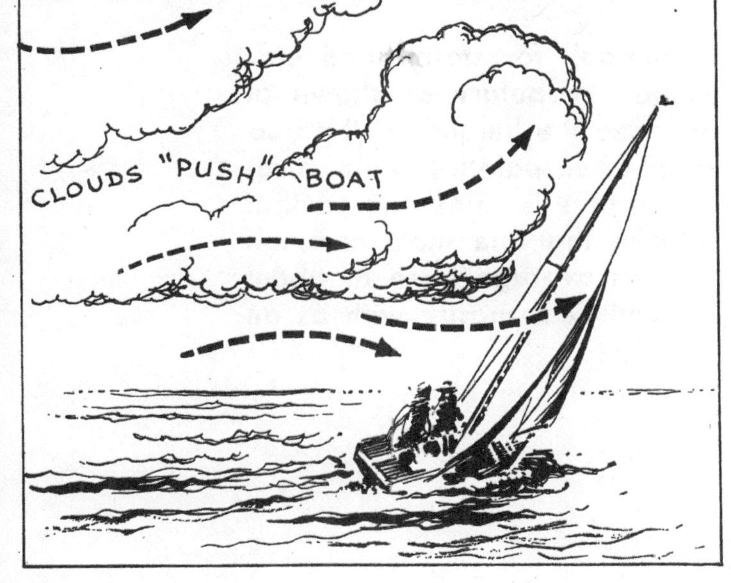

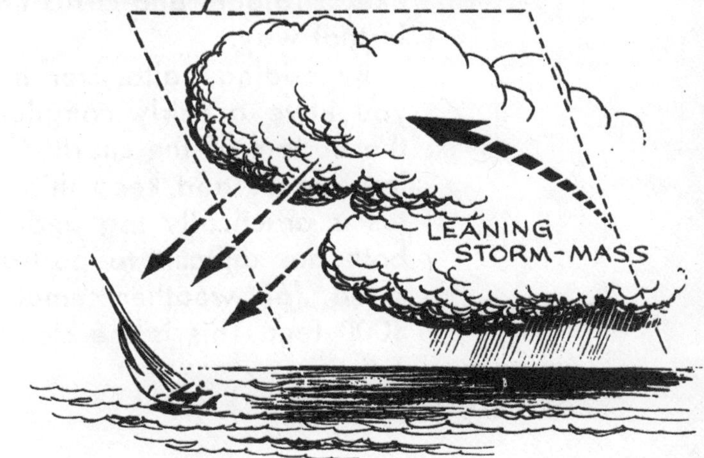

CLOUDS LEAN *or* "EXPLODE" WITH THE GENERAL ACTION OF YOUR PICTURE'S COMPOSITION

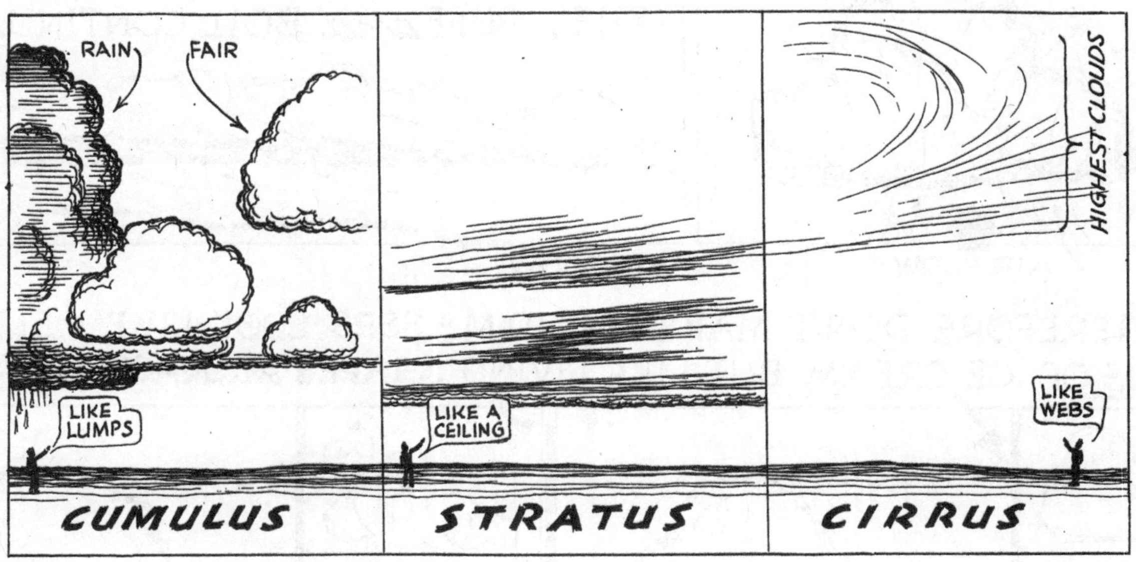

Now that you are aware of cloud action, let's learn some cloud nomenclature.

Because the following pages mention clouds by name, you might want to know what those names mean. Actually there are only three kinds of clouds although you will hear of very many Latin sounding names in meteorology. Anatomically speaking there is 1. CUMULUS, 2. STRATUS and 3. CIRRUS, as shown on the opposite page. Notice first, the man puffing a "cumulus" shape, the cigarette smoke forming a "stratus" layer across the room and the shapeless "cirrus" wisps seeping from the refrigerator. Learning these names is simple for cumulus sounds like the word "accumulated", stratus sounds like "straight" and cirrus has an "icy" sound. Memorize them in that way.

By adding "alto" for high, "nimbo" for storm-head etc., you have a fairly complete cloud vocabulary as shown at the bottom of the chart. You may see the heights of the various clouds and keep this in mind when painting them. Stratus is practically fog and nimbo stratus is rainy fog so that both are difficult to portray. Notice that the most common cloud, fair weather cumulus, has its average base at about 4000 feet. This is the cloud you will deal mostly with as an artist.

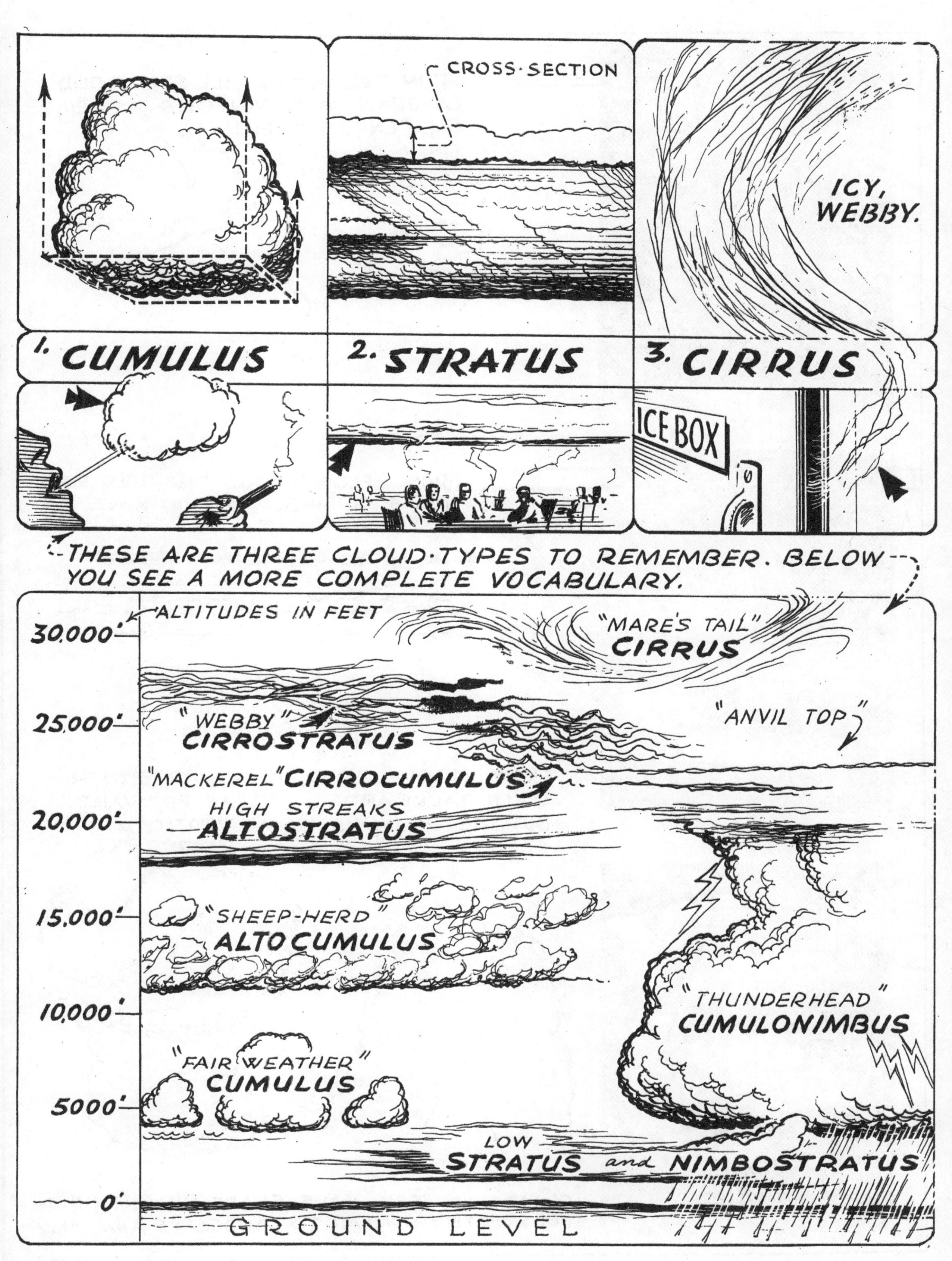
CROSS·SECTION
ICY, WEBBY.
1. CUMULUS
2. STRATUS
3. CIRRUS
ICE BOX
THESE ARE THREE CLOUD·TYPES TO REMEMBER. BELOW YOU SEE A MORE COMPLETE VOCABULARY.
ALTITUDES IN FEET
30,000'
25,000'
20,000'
15,000'
10,000'
5000'
0'
"MARE'S TAIL" CIRRUS
"WEBBY" CIRROSTRATUS
"ANVIL TOP"
"MACKEREL" CIRROCUMULUS
HIGH STREAKS ALTOSTRATUS
"SHEEP-HERD" ALTOCUMULUS
"THUNDERHEAD" CUMULONIMBUS
"FAIR WEATHER" CUMULUS
LOW STRATUS and NIMBOSTRATUS
GROUND LEVEL

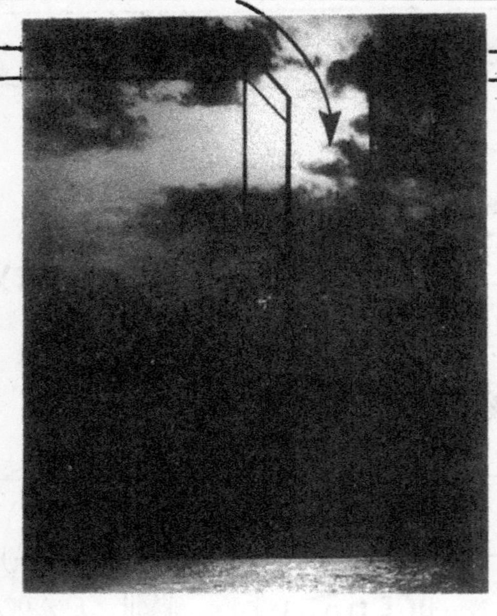

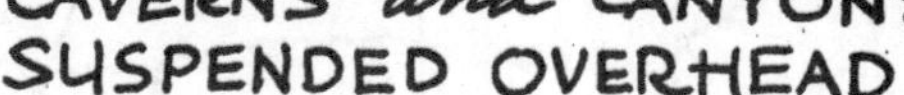

FROM BELOW, YOU WILL SEE CLOUD CAVERNS *and* CANYONS AS BEING SUSPENDED OVERHEAD

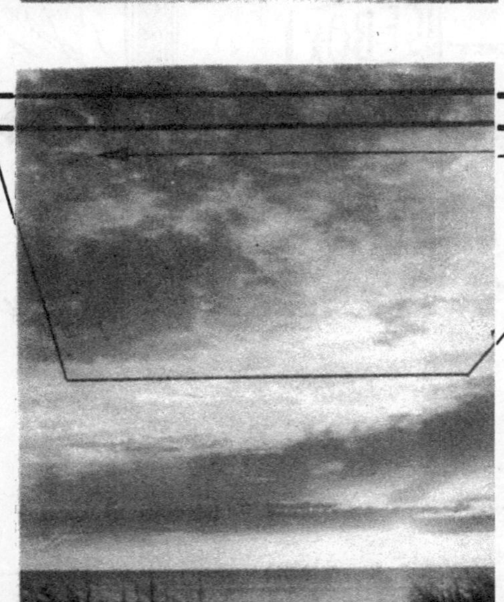

FROM BELOW, CLOUD PRAIRIES LOOK LIKE A CEILING *and* THEY HAVE PERSPECTIVE

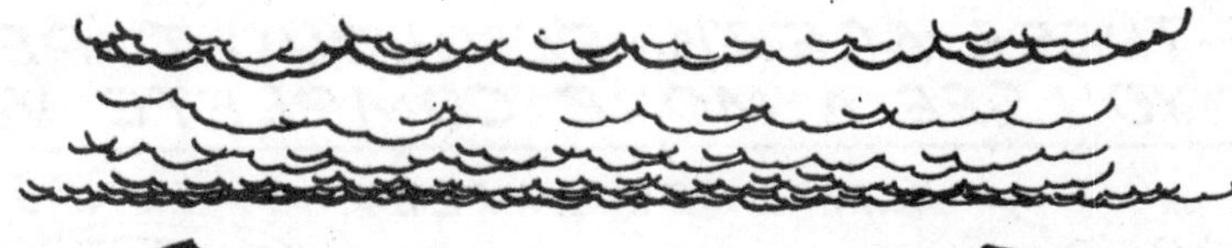

FROM BELOW, CLOUD MOUNTAINS EITHER "LEAN BACKWARD" *or* "LEAN FORWARD" BUT THE FEELING IS ALWAS VERTICAL

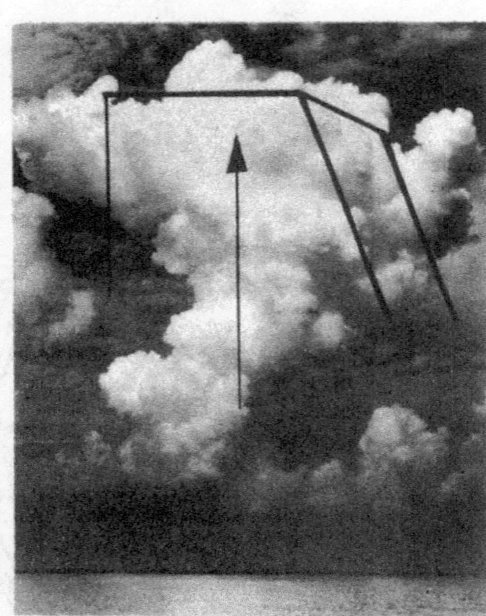

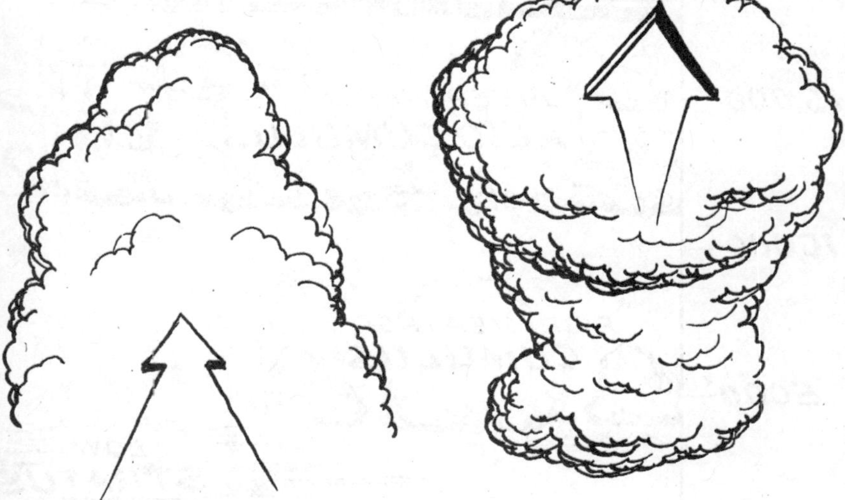

CLOUDS YOU SEE, HAVE SHAPE, DIMENSION *and* PERSPECTIVE SIMILAR TO LANDSCAPE ANATOMY

IN CLOUDLAND THERE ARE PRAIRIES, HILLS, CANYONS. THINKING OF CLOUDS IN THIS MANNER GIVES THE ARTIST THE SAME FREEDOM TO CREATE THAT EVERY LANDSCAPE PAINTER ENJOYS. LOOK AT THIS CANYON →

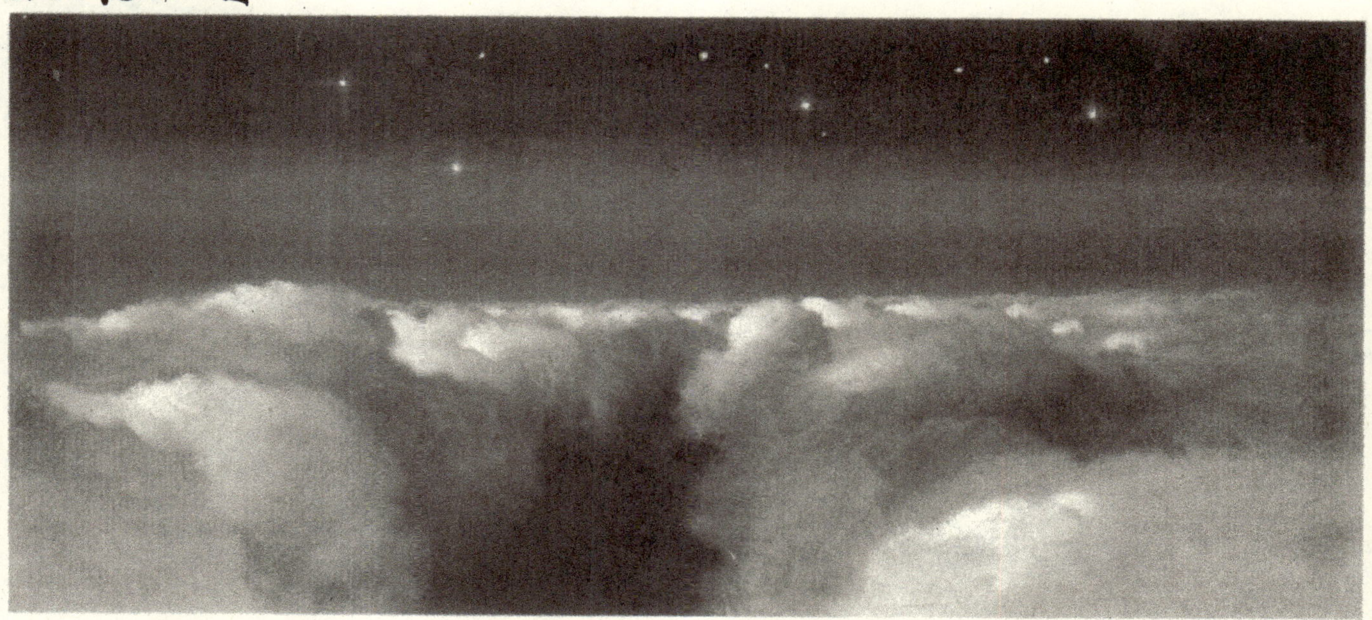

PRAIRIE →

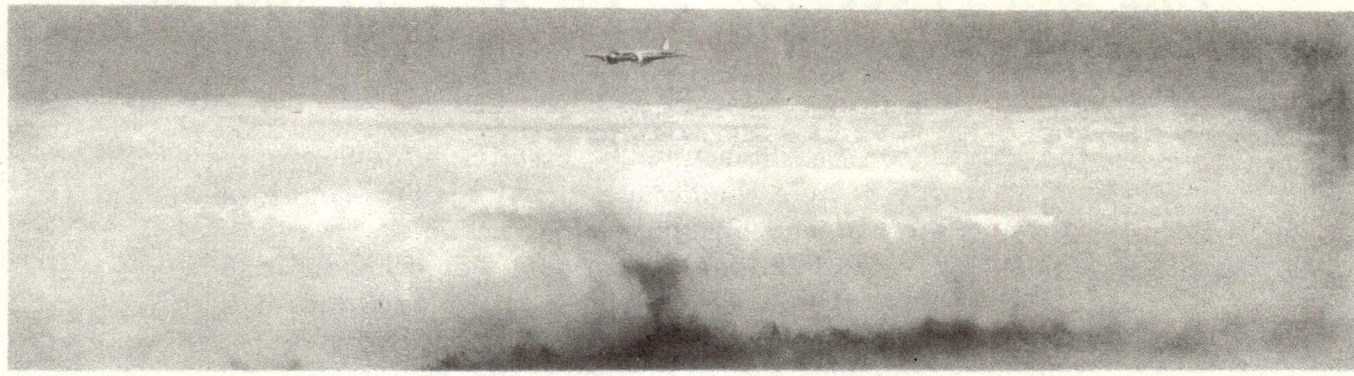

MOUNTAIN →

THERE'S EVERYTHING UP THERE THAT *the* LANDSCAPE HAS – AND MORE

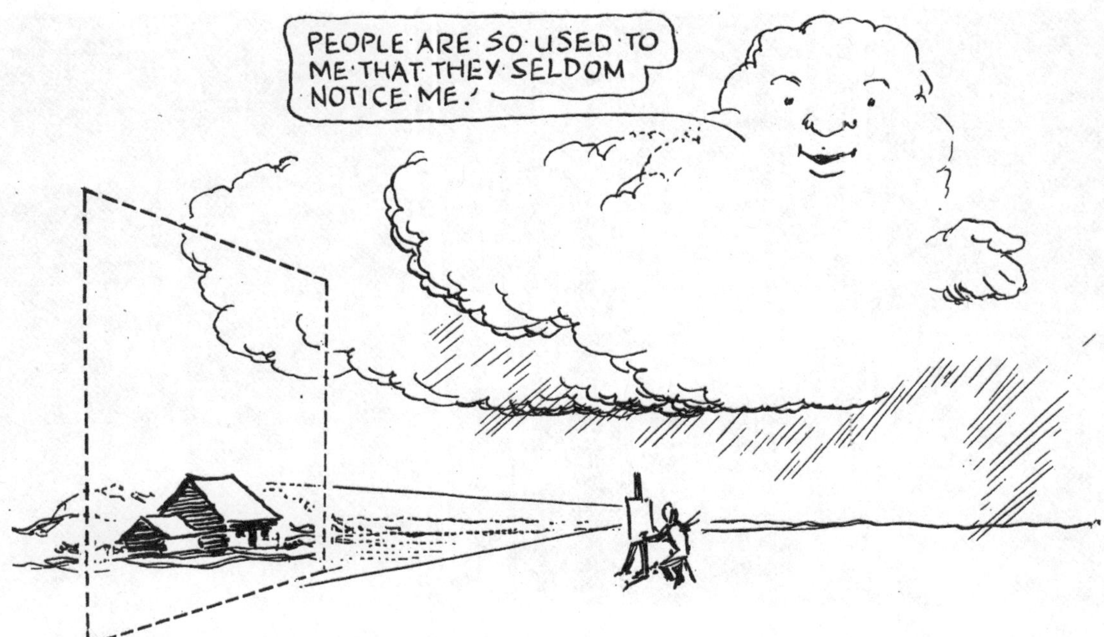

ARE SKIES ACCESSORIES OR SUBJECT MATTER?

Yes, clouds can be subjects or accessories. Whether landscape, seascape or pure cloudscape, the sky is the theatre of your picture's mood and backdrop of its action.

Opposite you see two landscapes: both would be dull and inexpressive without the sky. So true is this in fact, that it is difficult to tell whether the sky is subject or accessory.

Following, you will see a seascape and cloudscape. All three are done as charcoal sketches done on gray charcoal paper, using black Wolf pencil and white Nupastel. While learning to draw the sky it is wise to first sketch in black and white and leave the colors until sky anatomy has been mastered.

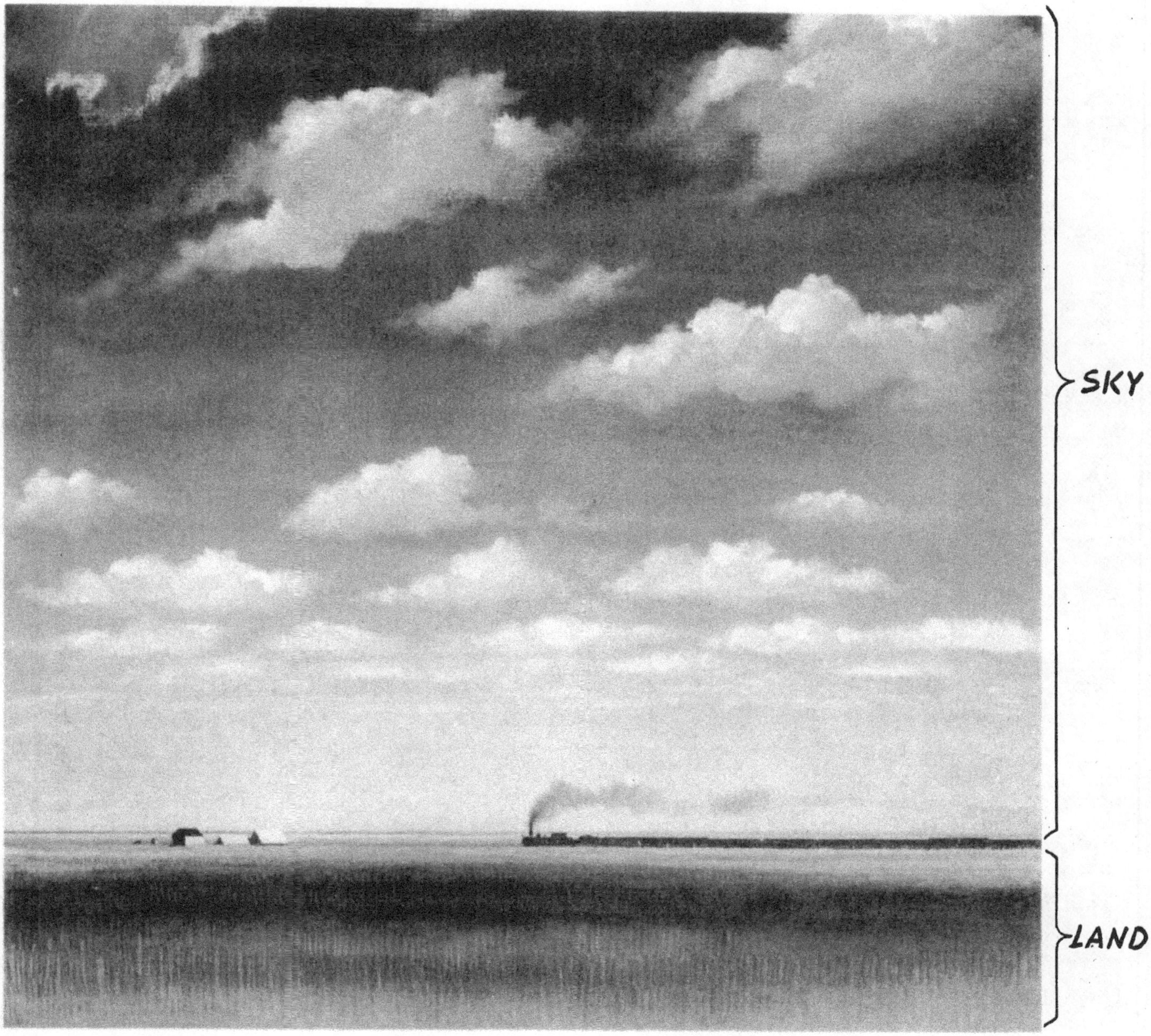

SKY

LAND

ABOVE, YOU SEE A "LANDSCAPE". OR IS IT? LET'S THINK OF IT AS A <u>CLOUDSCAPE</u>. HOW COULD *an* ARTIST ATTEMPT SUCH A PICTURE WITHOUT A KNOWLEDGE OF SKY-ANATOMY? EVEN WITH LESS SKY THE SKY COMMANDS *the* MOOD *and* EXTENT *of* ALL LANDSCAPES

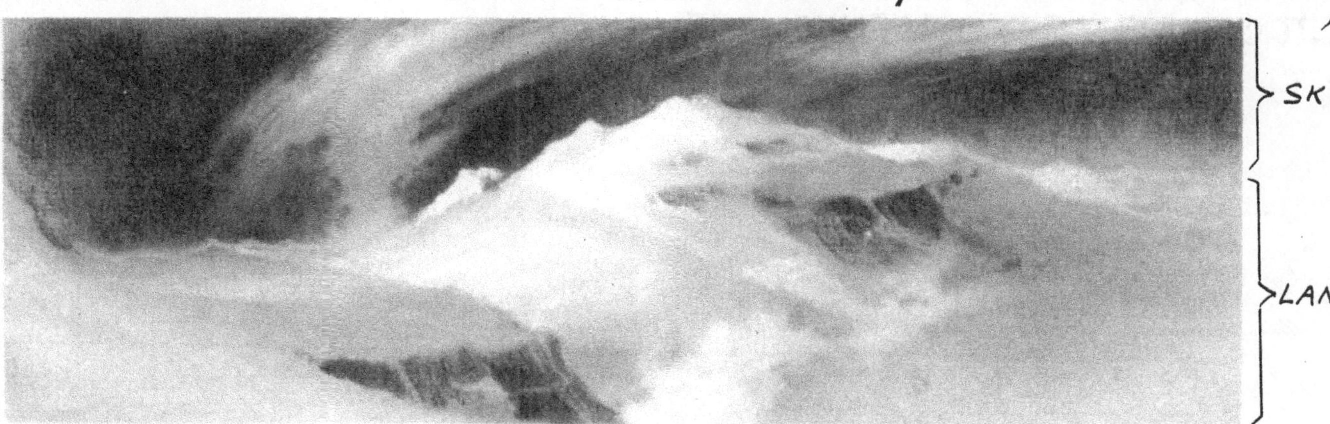

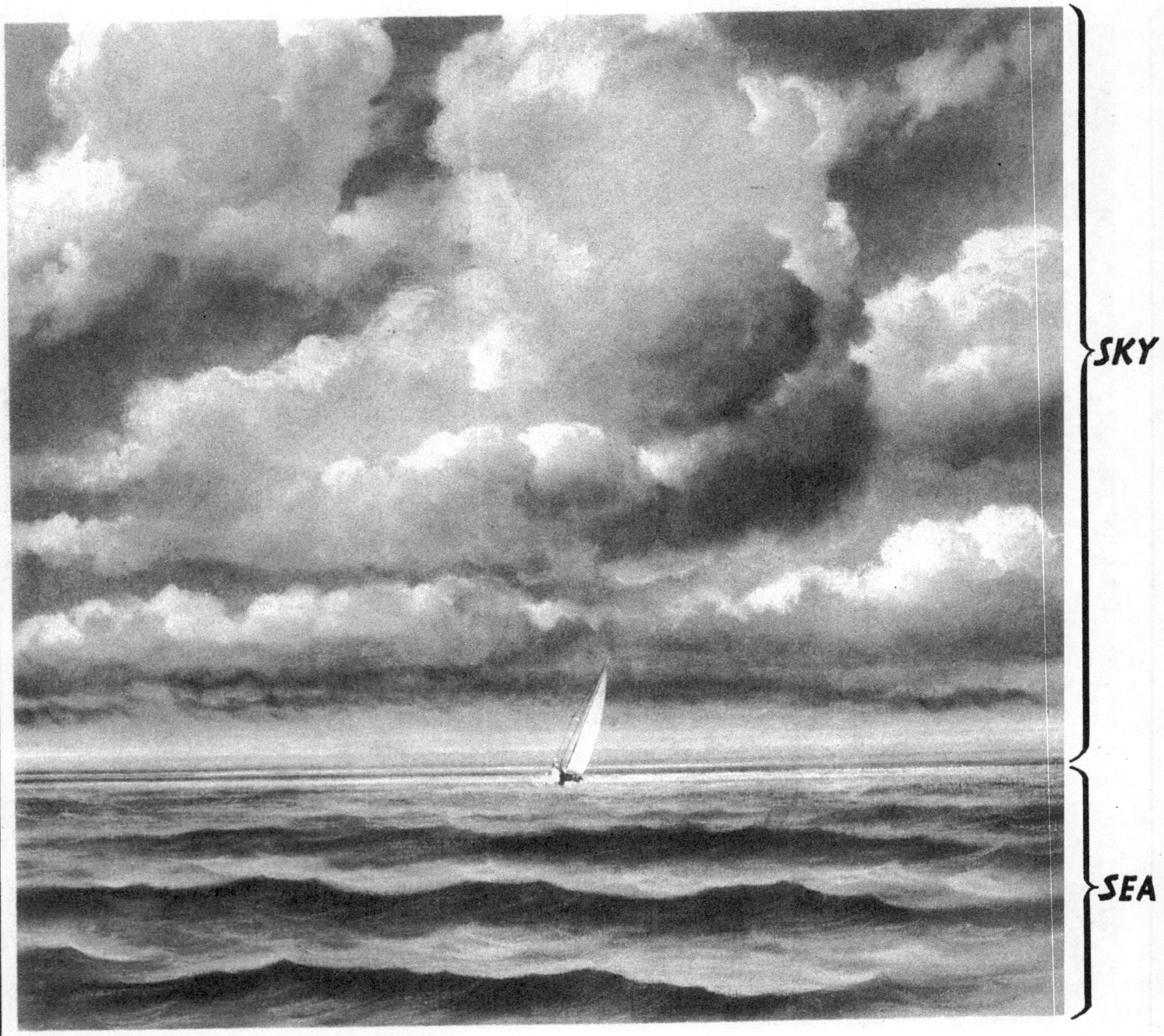

SKY

SEA

YOU WILL NOT FIND THE WORD "CLOUDSCAPE" IN THE DICTIONARY. EVEN THE ART CRITIC WOULD CALL THE ABOVE SKETCH *a* SEASCAPE YET MOST OF ITS SPACE *and* POWER IS IN ITS SKY. IT IS REALLY *a* CLOUDSCAPE! THE HORIZON IS USUALLY THOUGHT OF AS AN EARTH-MEASUREMENT. —IT IS ALSO A SKY-MEASUREMENT.

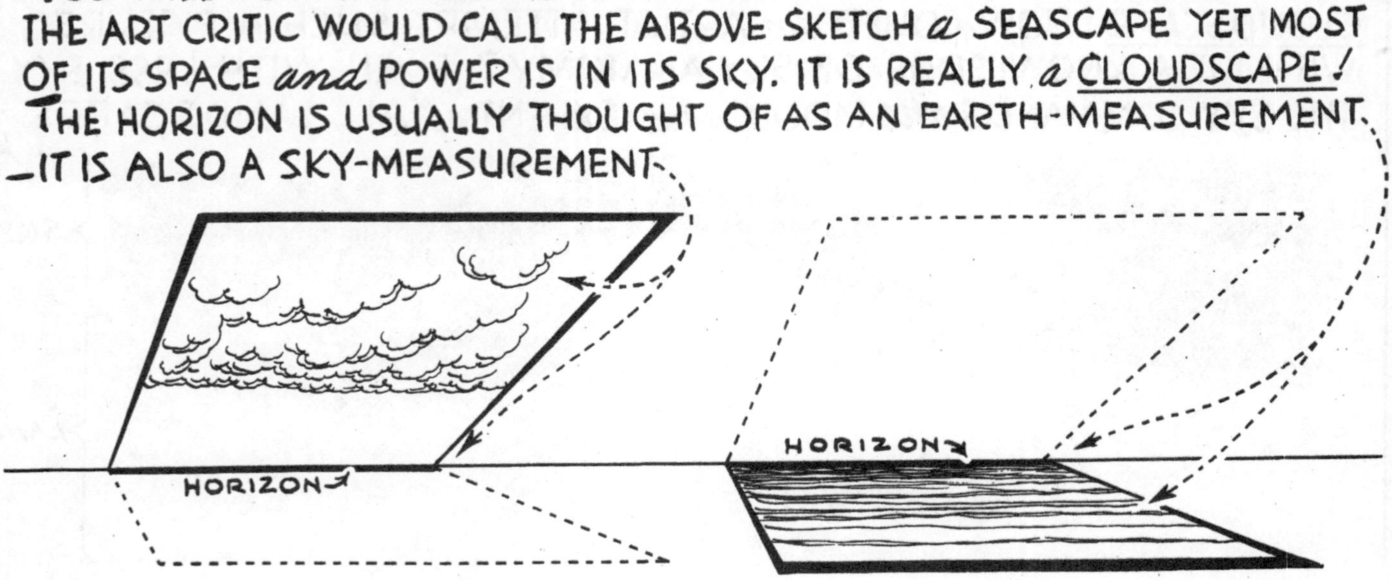

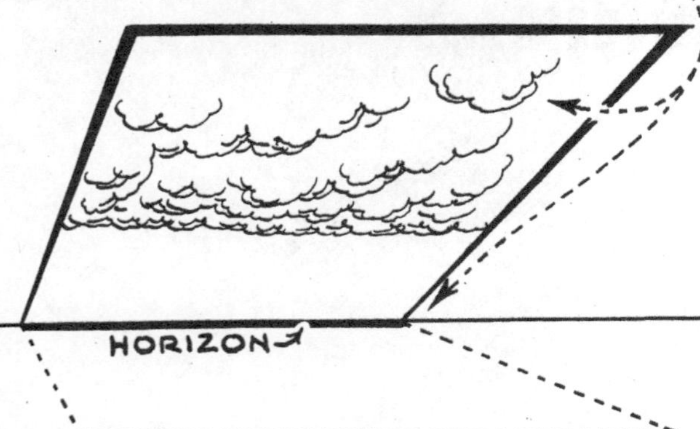

HORIZON

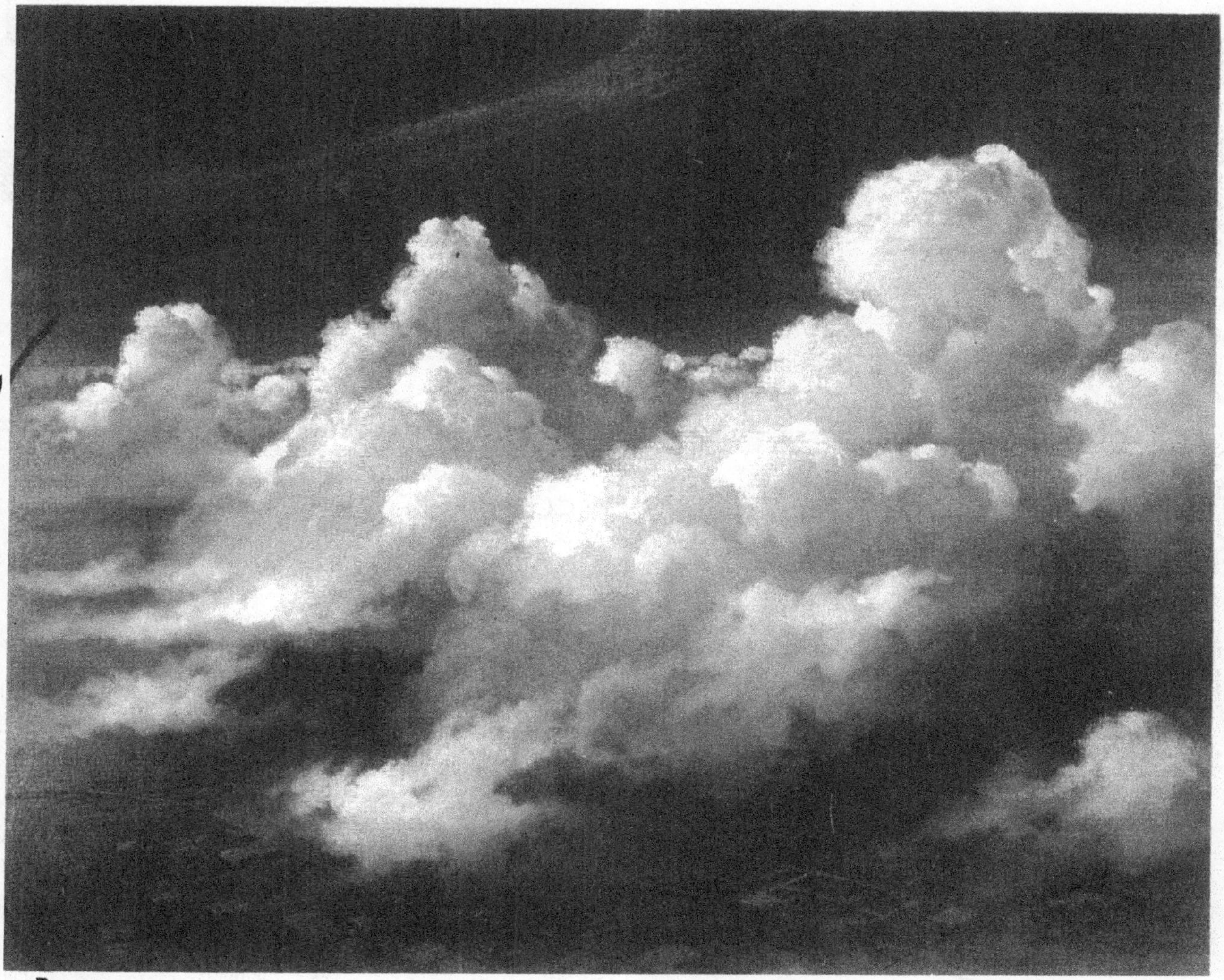

THIS IS INDEED A CLOUDSCAPE. LOOKING DOWN AT CLOUDS MAY NOT BE A POPULAR SUBJECT ANGLE BUT EACH DAY OF THIS FLYING AGE BRINGS US NEARER TO FEELING AT HOME AMONG *the* CLOUDS.

WE ARE AS YET UNACCUSTOMED TO SEEING CLOUD PICTURES WITH-OUT *a* PLANE. BY MAKING YOUR PLANE SMALL, YOUR CLOUDS WILL LOOM UP

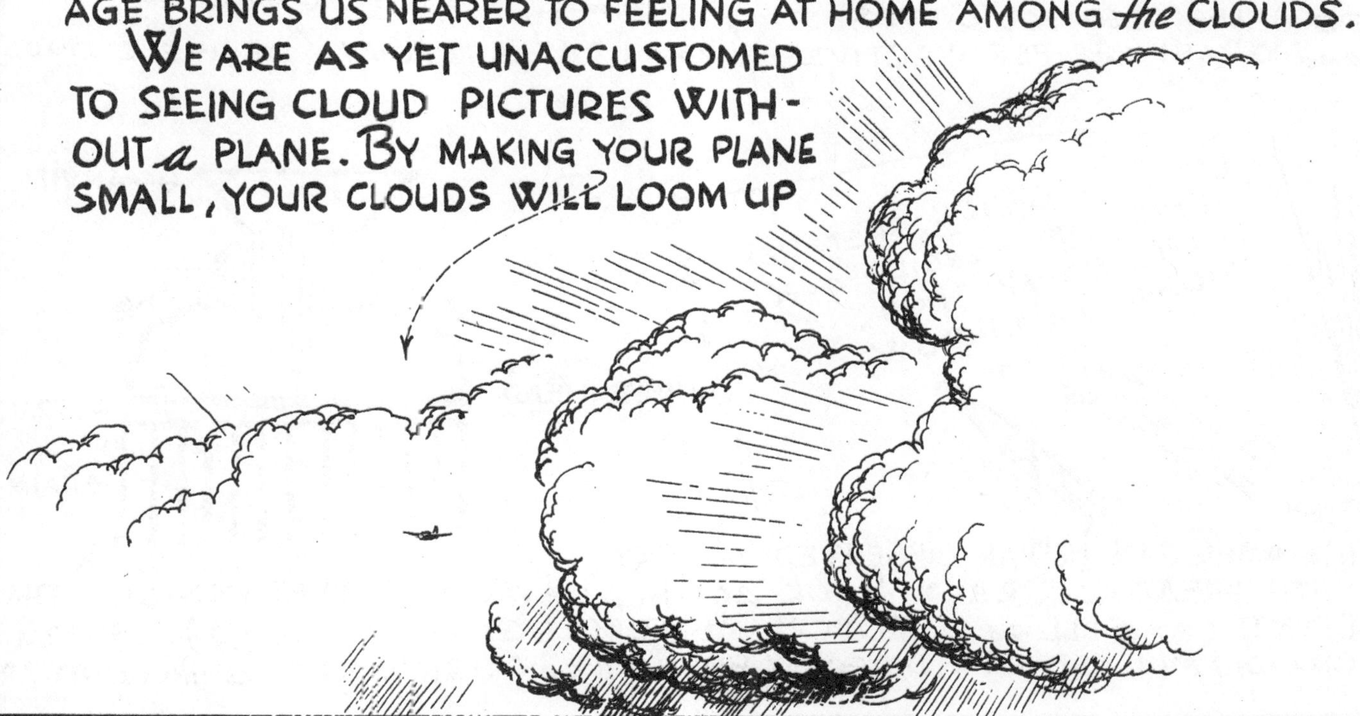

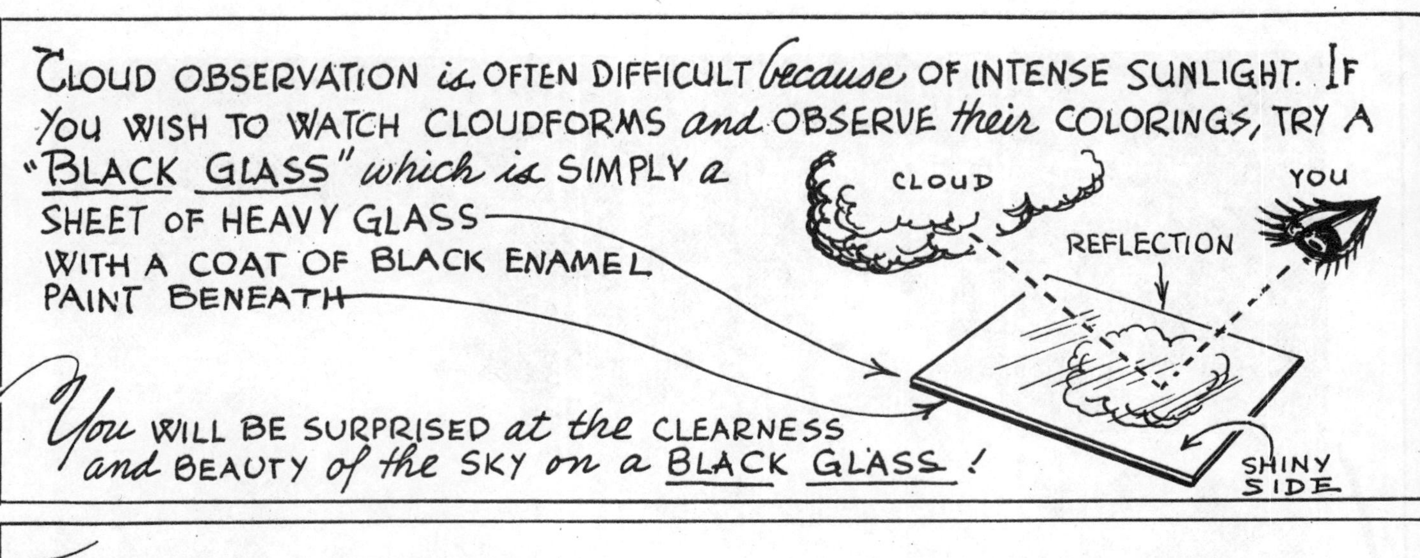

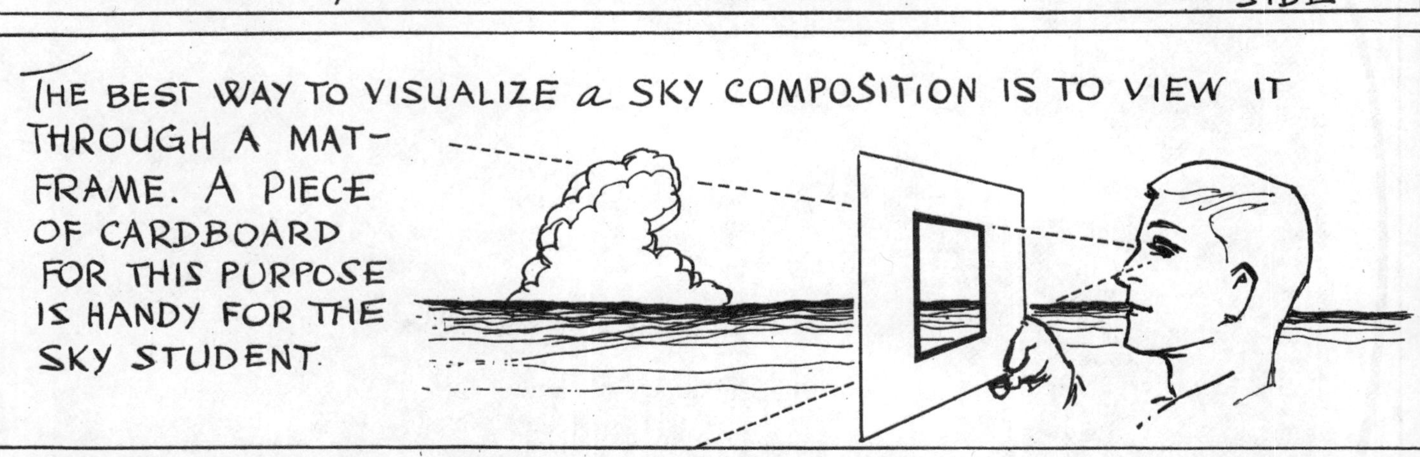

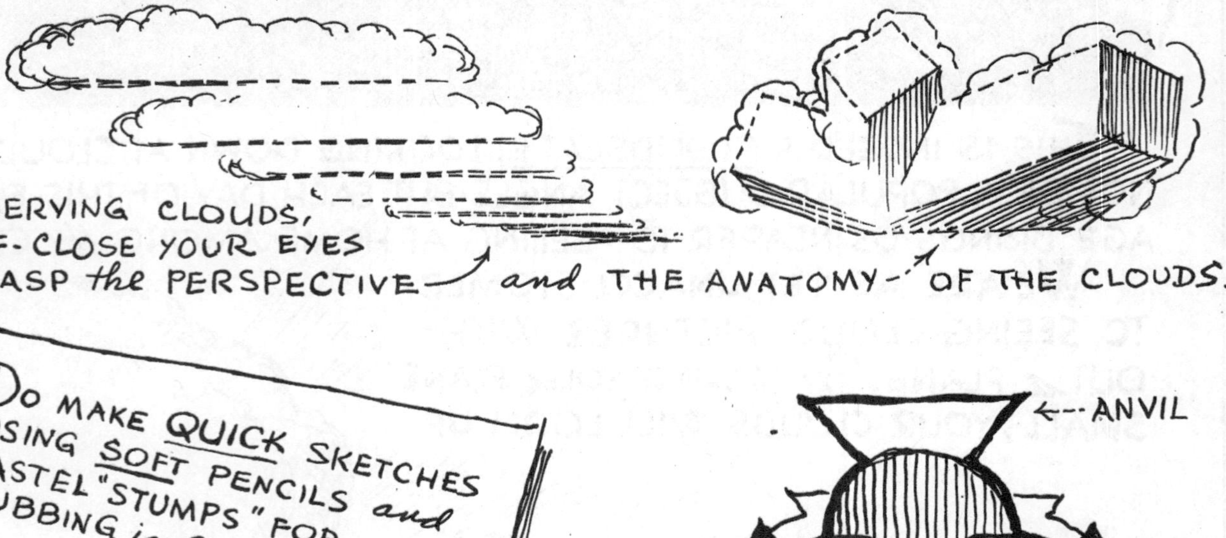

IN OBSERVING CLOUDS, DO HALF-CLOSE YOUR EYES and GRASP the PERSPECTIVE and THE ANATOMY OF THE CLOUDS.

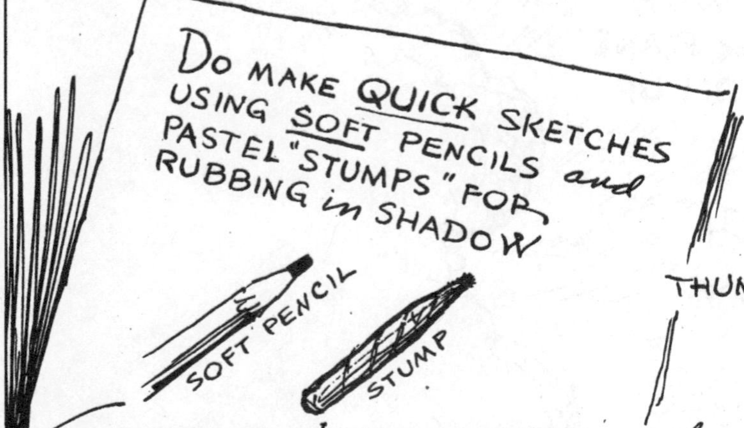

DO MAKE QUICK SKETCHES USING SOFT PENCILS and PASTEL "STUMPS" FOR RUBBING in SHADOW

SOFT PENCIL

STUMP

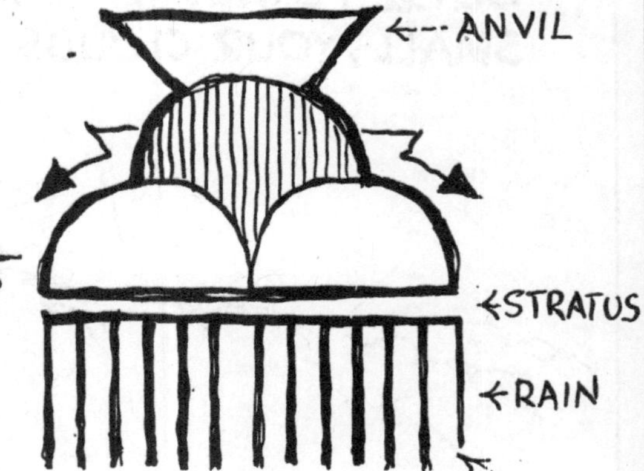

THUNDERHEAD

ANVIL

STRATUS

RAIN

THE AMERICAN INDIAN OBSERVED the SKY WITH GREAT ACCURACY. LOOK at THIS NAVAJO BLANKET DESIGN THAT DEPICTS (AS WELL as a MODERN METEOROLOGY BOOK WOULD) A STORM-CLOUD, ANVIL-TOP, RAIN DIRECTLY BENEATH and LIGHTNING FLASHING OUTWARD.

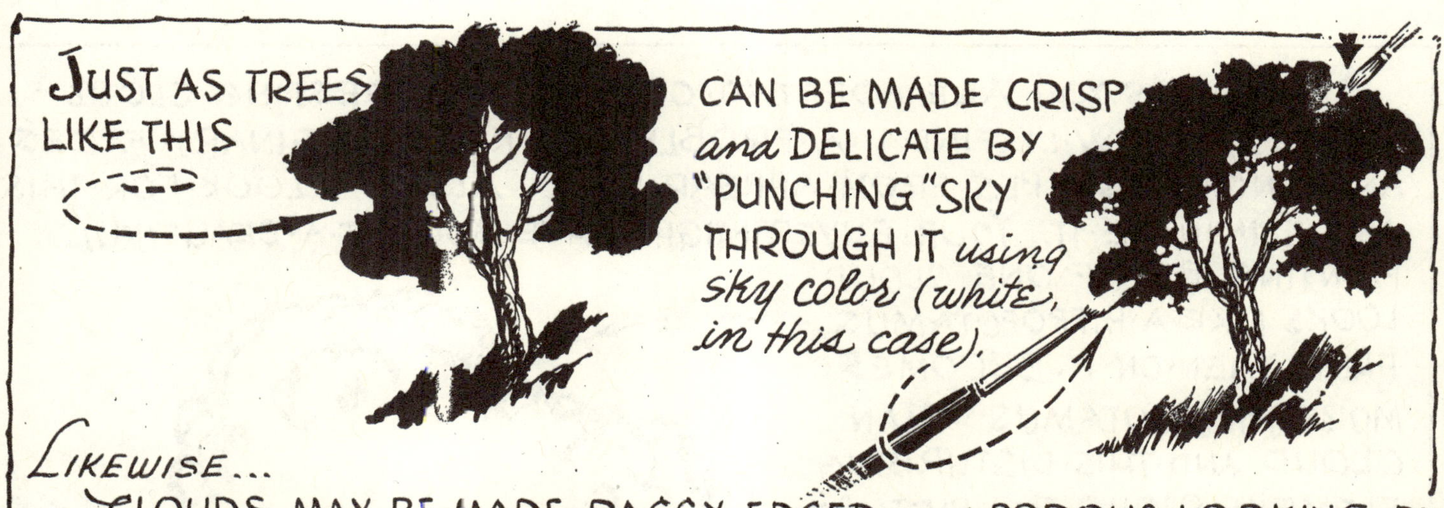

LIKEWISE...

.....CLOUDS MAY BE MADE RAGGY-EDGED and POROUS-LOOKING BY "EATING" INTERESTING HOLES and EDGES THROUGH THEM WITH SAME COLOR and TONE AS THE REST OF THE SKY. HERE IS a PHOTOGRAPH of RAGGED "SCUD" or CLOUD-REMNANT. BELOW are TWO TREATMENTS; FIRST, JUST "CLOUD-OVER-BLUE-SKY"; SECOND DRAWING has **SKY-HOLES** PUNCHED THROUGH. NOTICE the CRISP and PROFESSIONAL TOUCH THIS GIVES!

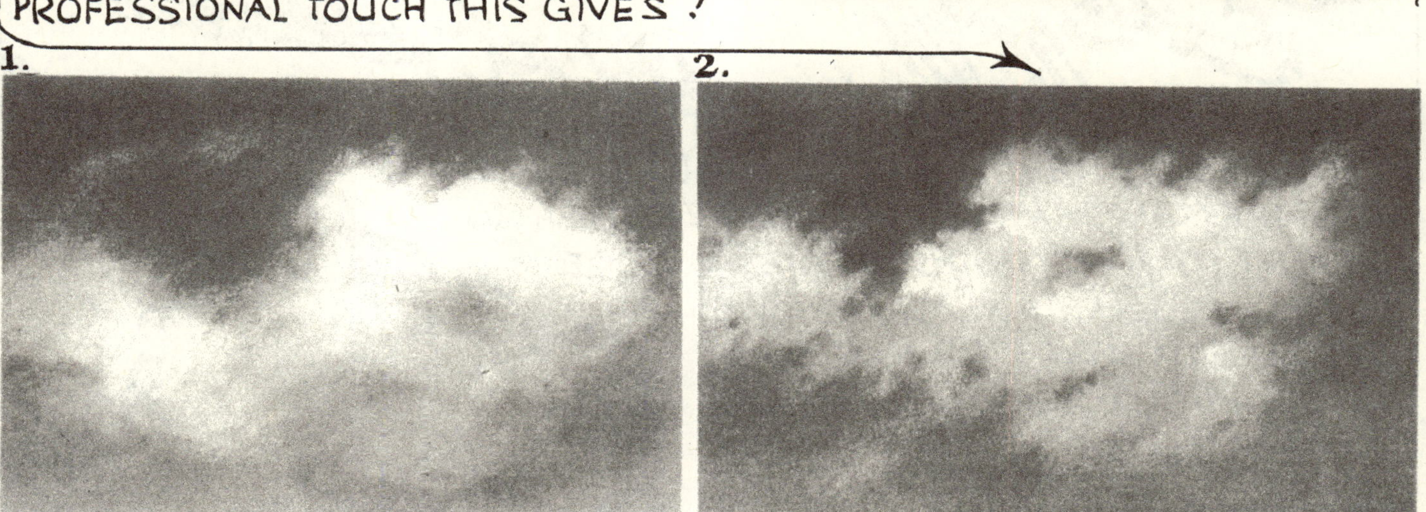

NOW LOOK BELOW and OBSERVE the CUT-IN EDGES(A) and the SKY-HOLES(B)

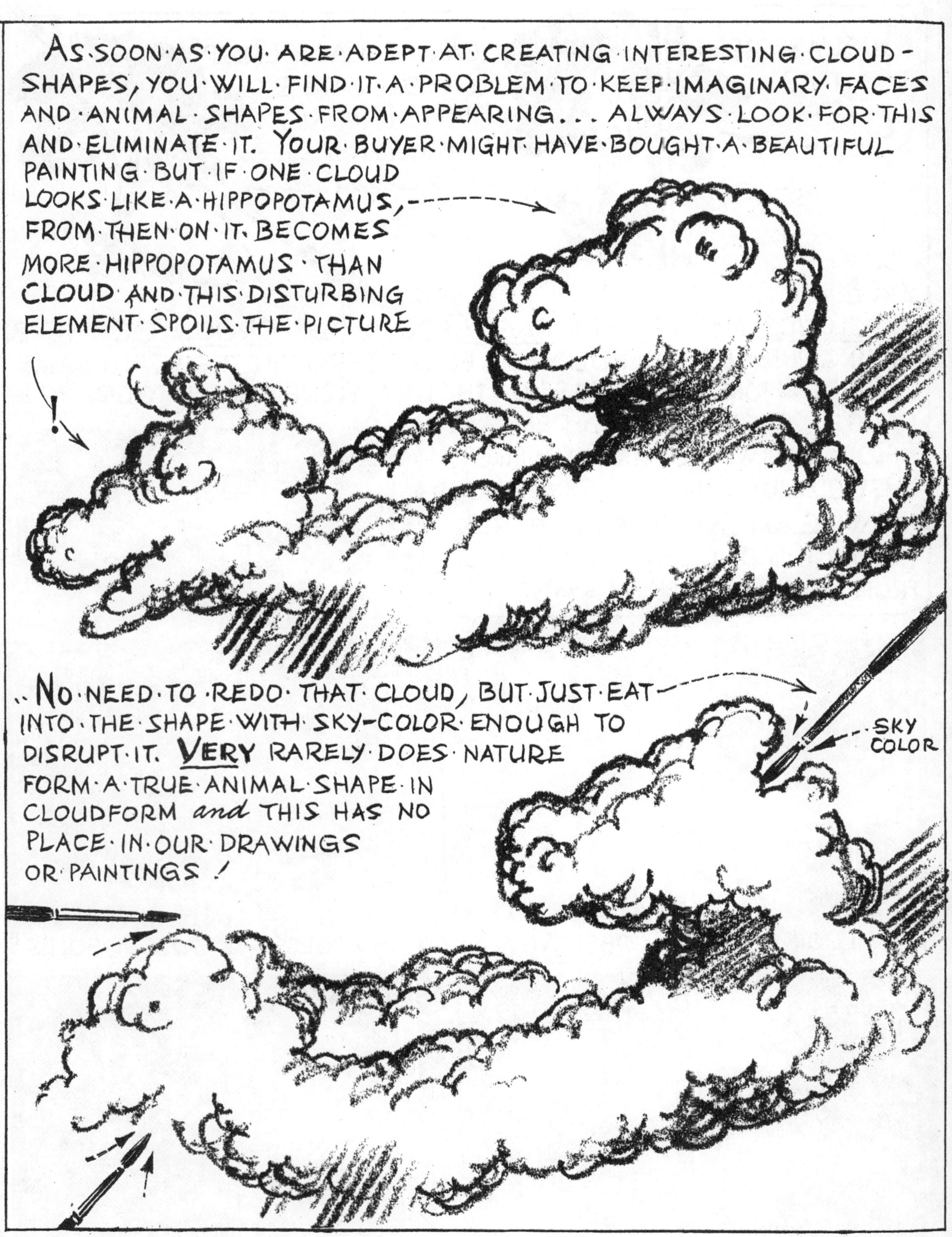
AS·SOON·AS·YOU·ARE·ADEPT·AT·CREATING·INTERESTING·CLOUD-SHAPES, YOU·WILL·FIND·IT·A·PROBLEM·TO·KEEP·IMAGINARY·FACES AND·ANIMAL·SHAPES·FROM·APPEARING... ALWAYS·LOOK·FOR·THIS AND·ELIMINATE·IT. YOUR·BUYER·MIGHT·HAVE·BOUGHT·A·BEAUTIFUL PAINTING·BUT·IF·ONE·CLOUD LOOKS·LIKE·A·HIPPOPOTAMUS, FROM·THEN·ON·IT·BECOMES MORE·HIPPOPOTAMUS·THAN CLOUD·AND·THIS·DISTURBING ELEMENT·SPOILS·THE·PICTURE
!
..NO·NEED·TO·REDO·THAT·CLOUD, BUT·JUST·EAT INTO·THE·SHAPE·WITH·SKY-COLOR·ENOUGH TO DISRUPT·IT. VERY RARELY·DOES·NATURE FORM·A·TRUE·ANIMAL·SHAPE·IN CLOUDFORM and THIS HAS NO PLACE·IN·OUR·DRAWINGS OR·PAINTINGS!
SKY COLOR

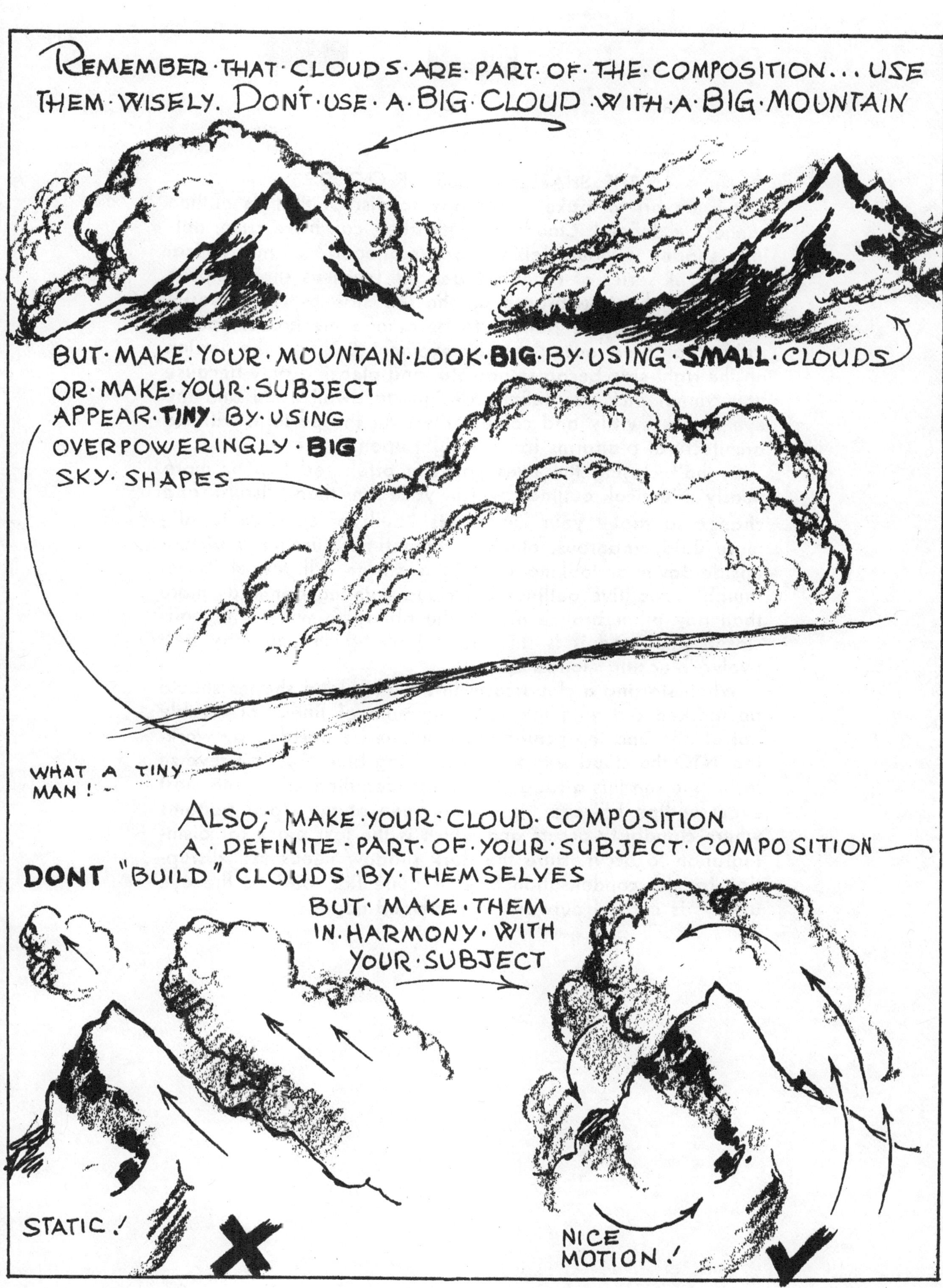
REMEMBER · THAT · CLOUDS · ARE · PART · OF · THE · COMPOSITION . . . USE
THEM · WISELY. DON'T · USE · A · BIG · CLOUD · WITH · A · BIG · MOUNTAIN
BUT · MAKE · YOUR · MOUNTAIN · LOOK · BIG · BY · USING · SMALL · CLOUDS
OR · MAKE · YOUR · SUBJECT
APPEAR · TINY · BY · USING
OVERPOWERINGLY · BIG
SKY · SHAPES
WHAT A TINY
MAN !
ALSO; MAKE · YOUR · CLOUD · COMPOSITION
A · DEFINITE · PART · OF · YOUR · SUBJECT · COMPOSITION
DONT "BUILD" CLOUDS BY THEMSELVES
BUT · MAKE · THEM
IN · HARMONY · WITH
YOUR · SUBJECT
STATIC !
NICE
MOTION !

THE SHAPELESSNESS OF CLOUDS.

It is an art to make any shape so disrupt that its outline cannot be defined. Clouds, as with trees, can have crisp, definite shapes without melting into "scalloped" or mechanical outlines. A series of repetitive designs (such as shown in the cloud and the tree branch on the left side of the opposite drawing) cause the pattern to become a mechanical detail rather than be a loose flow of movement. See how the portion on the right side becomes graceful and pleasing only because you cannot pick out definite designs to dwell upon and the eye moves swiftly and contentedly over the pattern, with no architectural platforms for it to light upon.

By half closing the eyes you can often see two or more nearly identical outlines which you can then disrupt and change to make your cloud less "built of solid material", more fluid, vaporous, ethereal. Sometimes turning a picture upside-down or looking at it in a mirror will reveal "sore-thumb" repetitive outlines but cloud-painting demands more than any other branch of art, the ability to work with half-closed eyes and it is this method by which you may best evolve pleasing cloudshapes.

When starting a cloudscape in oils the cloud shapes should be marked out with the very minimum of lines (preferably not at all) and the actual cloud outline be decided by working INTO the cloud with the surrounding blue sky. This reverse technique renders a ragged and less identified edge. The most exact outline however, is usually seen at the cloud bottoms where cloudbirth occurs and which is the last place for disintegration to occur. Here the dark shadow needs less disruption for the condensation level is quite flat, besides the eye always is carried outward to the cloud-edges.

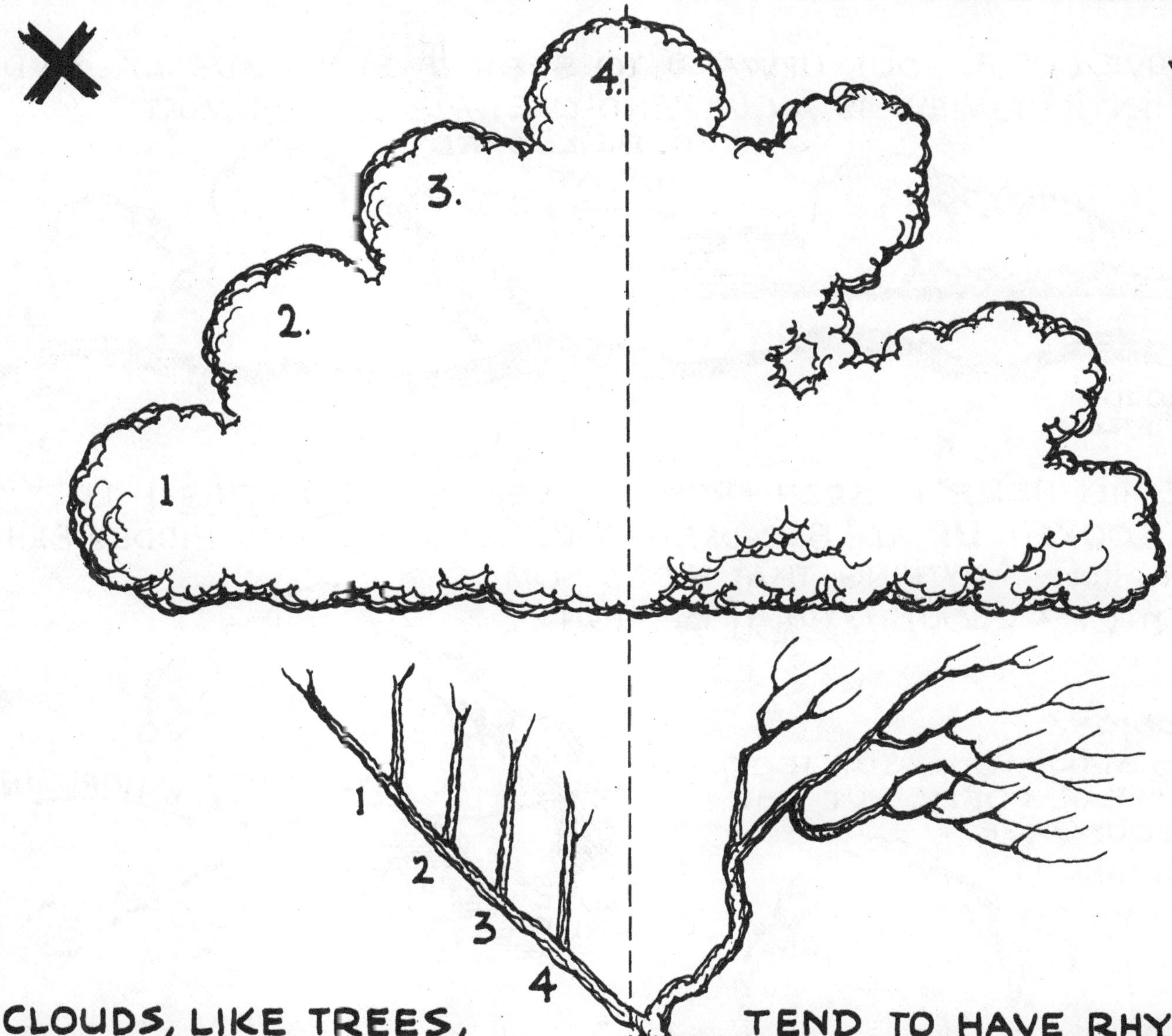

CLOUDS, LIKE TREES, TEND TO HAVE RHYTHM WITHOUT REPETITION. MONOTONOUS PATTERNS SHOULD BE DISRUPTED TO AVOID ATTENTION-GETTING "SORE THUMB" SHAPES. BY SQUINTING *the* EYES YOU MAY PICK OUT REPETITIVE DESIGNS *and* ELIMINATE THEM

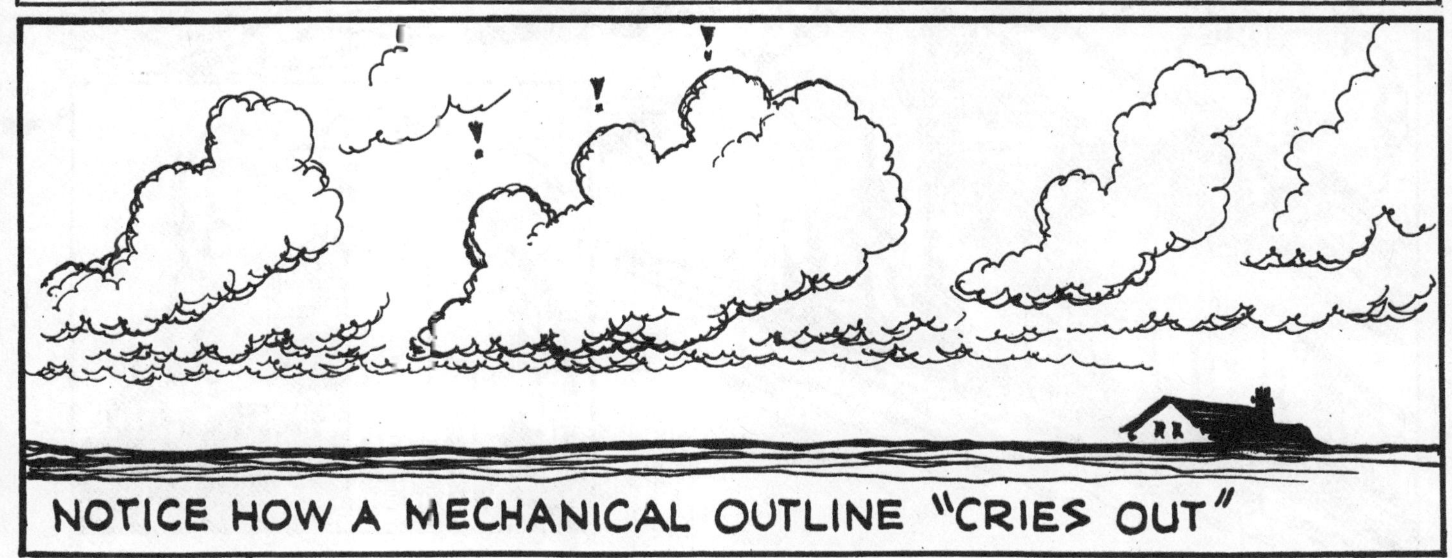

NOTICE HOW A MECHANICAL OUTLINE "CRIES OUT"

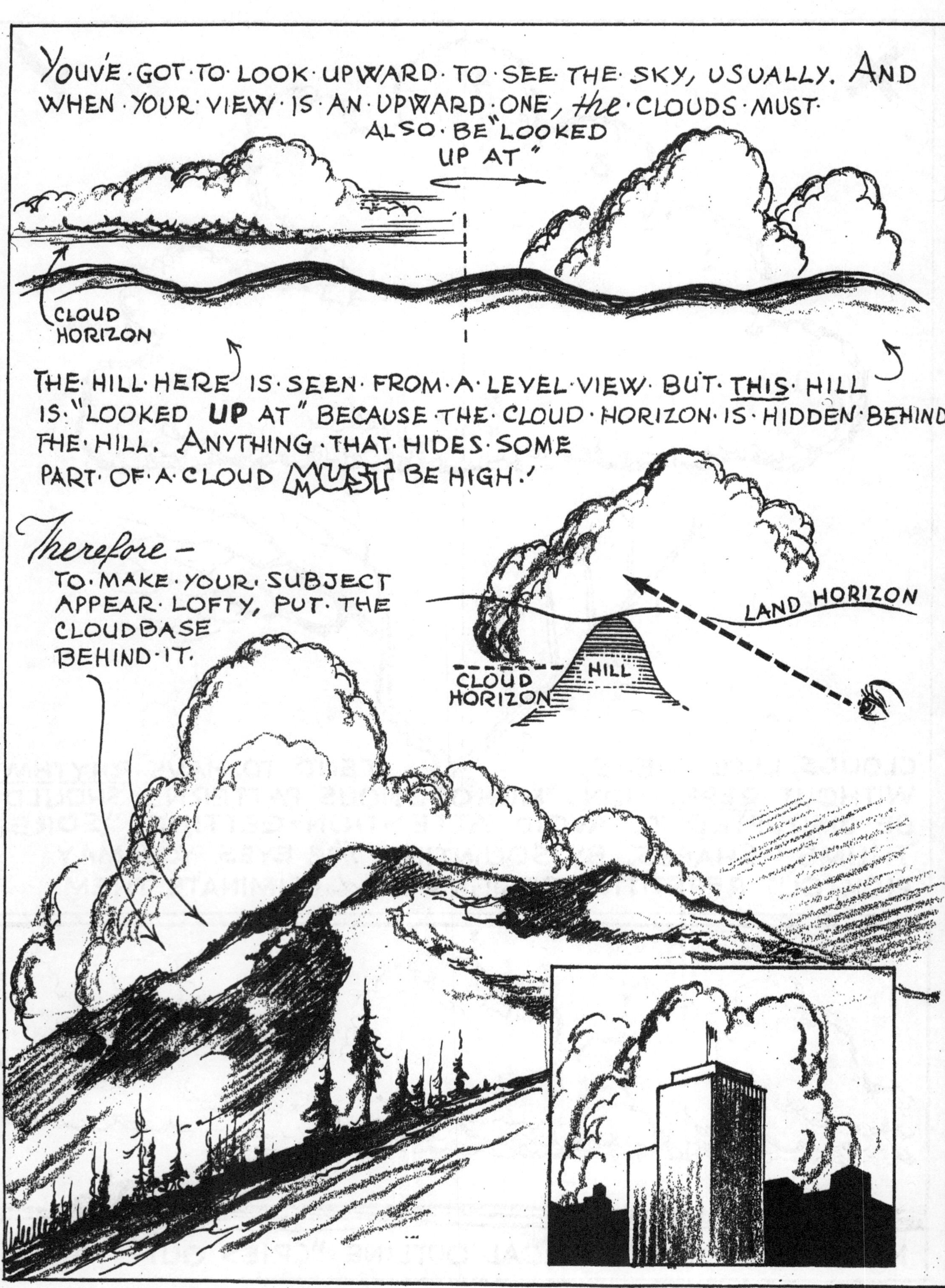
YOU'VE · GOT · TO · LOOK · UPWARD · TO · SEE · THE · SKY, USUALLY. AND WHEN · YOUR · VIEW · IS · AN · UPWARD · ONE, *the* · CLOUDS · MUST · ALSO · BE "LOOKED UP AT"
CLOUD HORIZON
THE · HILL · HERE IS · SEEN · FROM · A · LEVEL · VIEW · BUT · THIS · HILL IS "LOOKED UP AT" BECAUSE · THE · CLOUD · HORIZON · IS · HIDDEN · BEHIND THE · HILL. ANYTHING · THAT · HIDES · SOME PART · OF · A · CLOUD MUST BE HIGH!
Therefore -
TO · MAKE · YOUR · SUBJECT APPEAR · LOFTY, PUT · THE CLOUDBASE BEHIND · IT.
LAND HORIZON
HILL
CLOUD HORIZON

CLOUDS ARE SOMETIMES MOUNTAINS... PAINT THEM AS SUCH AND YOU CAN ACHIEVE *the* AWE *and* MAJESTY OF LOFTY MOUNTAIN PEAKS. BELOW YOU SEE A MOUNTAIN SKETCH, ROUGHLY MASSING *the* LIGHTS AND SHADOWS TO LAY OUT *an* INTERESTING COMPOSITION →

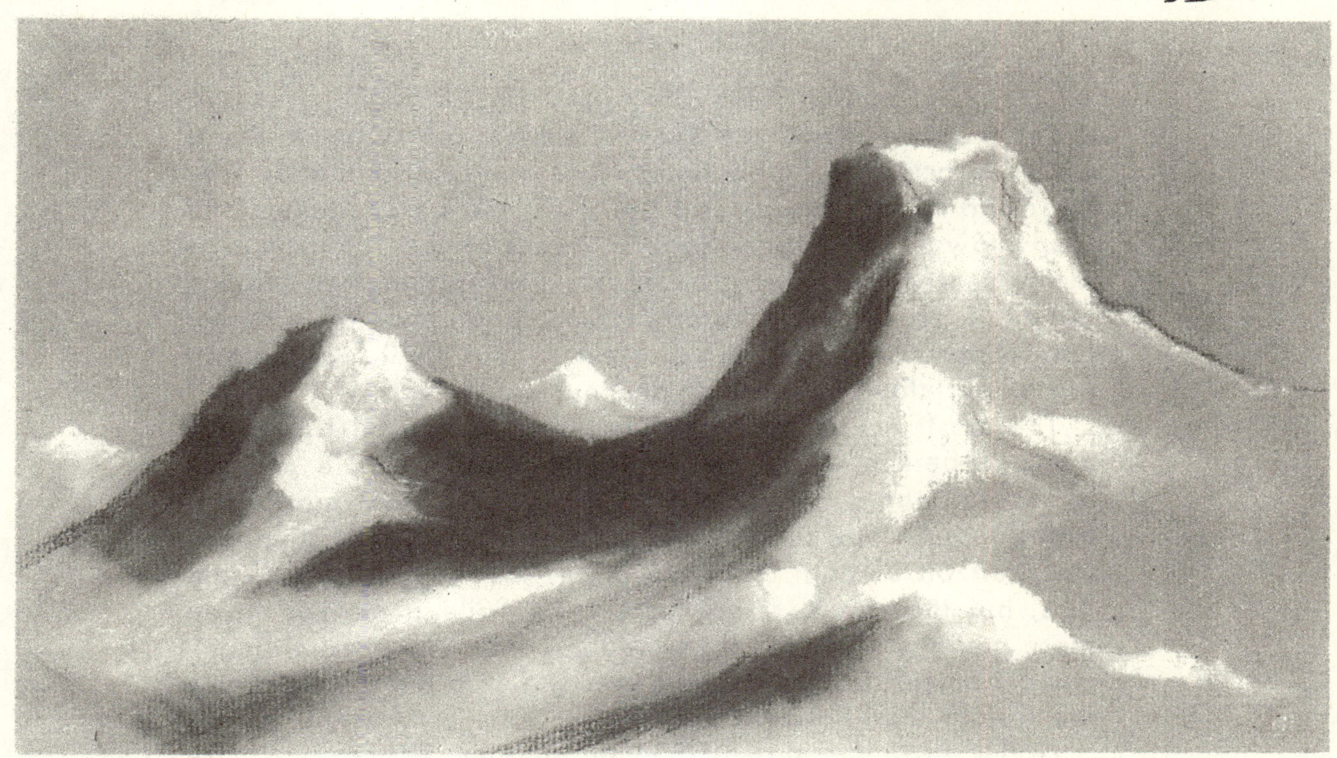

THIS COMPOSITION MAY BE PUT INTO CLOUDFORM. **NEVER** SEE OUTLINES LIKE THIS → BUT SEE MASSES ALONE, LIKE THIS → AND

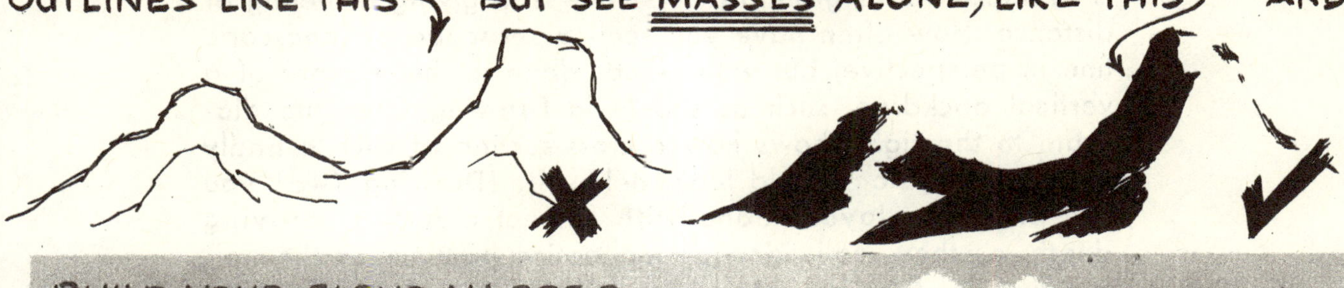

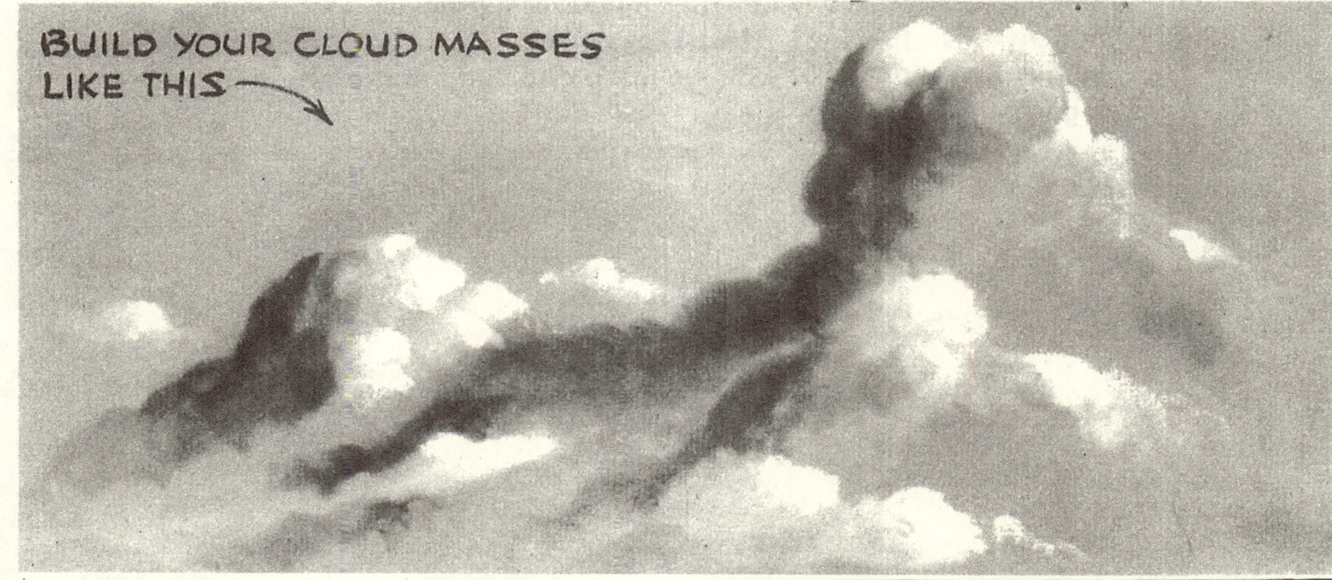

THE ANATOMY OF CUMULUS CLOUDS.

On the next page you see a "prairie" of cumulus clouds with characteristic flat bottoms; it is windy and that is why the cloud-masses are spread out, flattened before they could really tower. The ragged-looking cloud in the foreground is in the process of disintegration, has broken into two, leaving behind a trail of fast disappearing remnants. The weather here is perfect and the clouds are at about 4500 feet, according to our cloud-knowledge and our cloud-chart.

The most interesting feature in this photograph is that the average person would call it a "landscape", while actually almost the entire composition is cloud-space! Next most interesting to the cloud student is the cloud-bank's perspective. The true horizon of both land and sky is just beyond the distant hills, but the clouds really have as definite a horizon, even more obvious a horizon than the land. This "inverted horizon" could be seen at sea or on perfectly flat ground, just above the distant land-horizon.

Notice how the masses become smaller, flatter, closer together with distance, until near the horizon where the effect becomes that of closely-knit horizontal lines. This phenomena is as important as ground perspective is in giving a feeling of distance. How often have you seen a seascape or landscape fine in perspective, but with clouds done in the manner of a vertical backdrop, such as shown in Drawing One: the diagram to the right shows how a cross-section of such a badly done composition would look. Below it, (Drawing Two) you see the same layout done with correct clouds portraying depth, as they really do appear; notice how better the perspective is, for both clouds and sea have their vanishing points now, as shown in the accompanying diagram at the right.

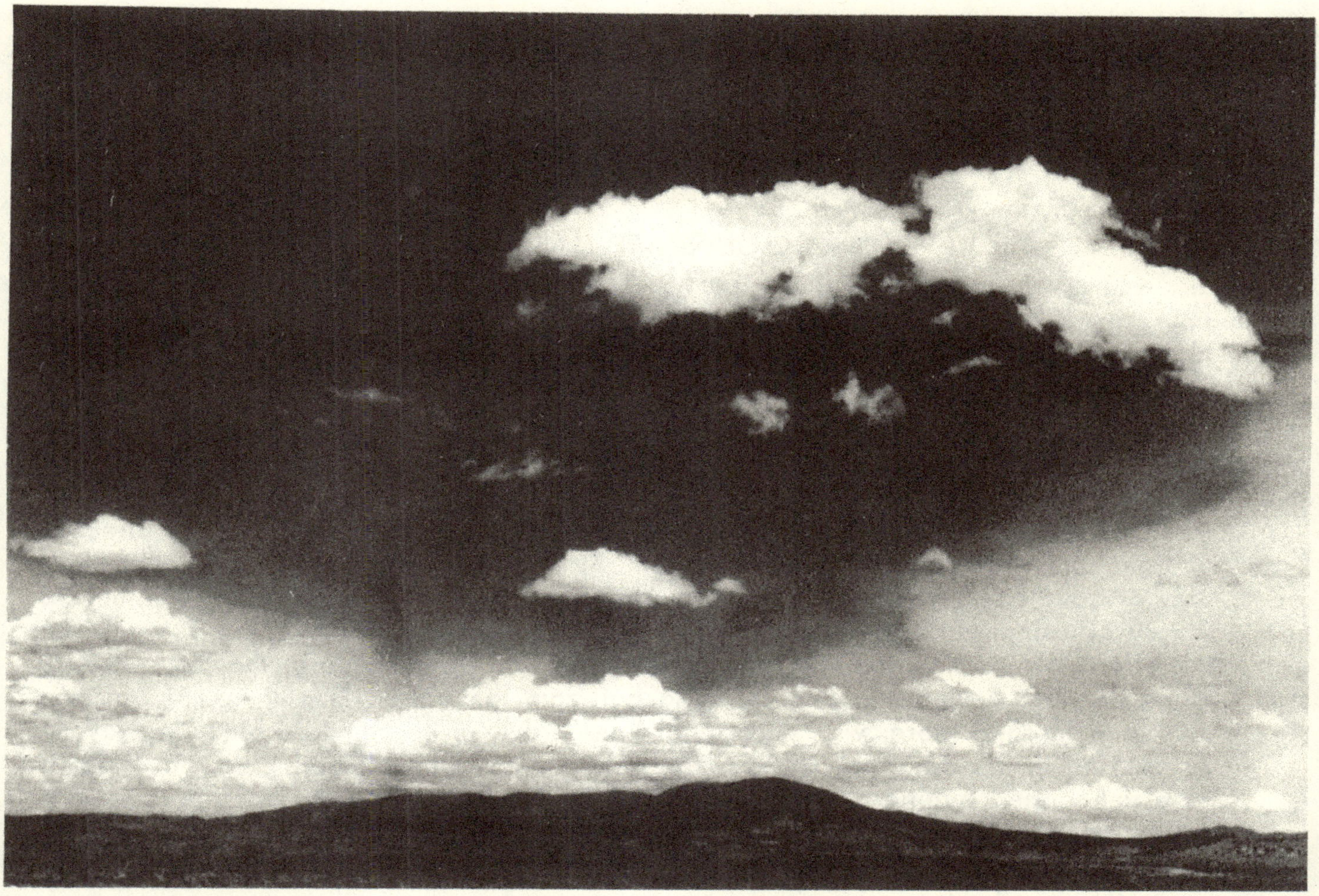

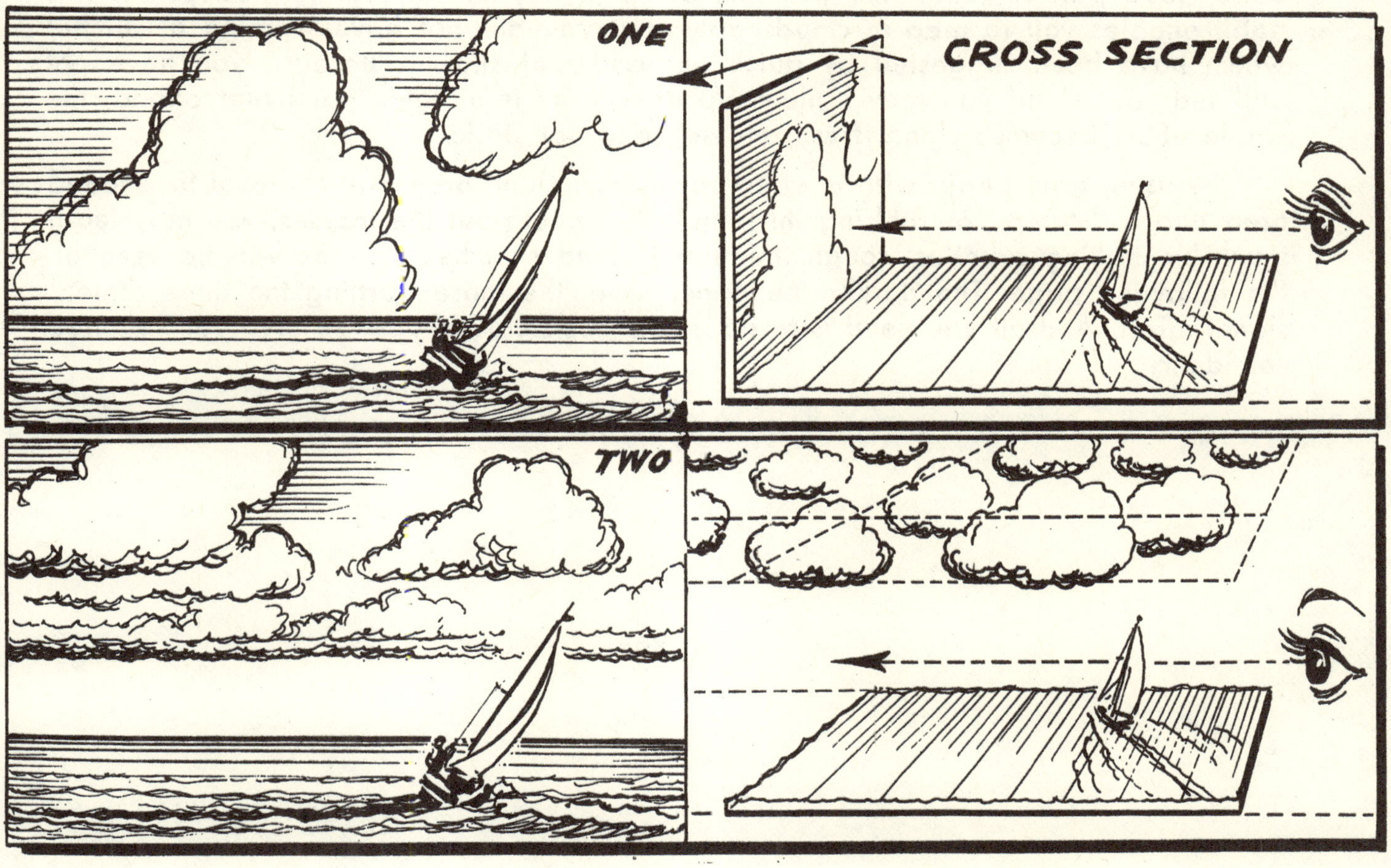

ONE

CROSS SECTION

TWO

CLOUDS ARE MASSES

The best way to paint a cloud is to block in the masses of light and dark, **avoiding outlines.** You will find that by working fast and with the eyes half closed, countless "happy accidents" will occur, some of which you may retain and build up: by outlining a cloud you immediately limit yourself and lose that freedom of creation while working out the cloudshape. In the drawing opposite, (A) shows a cloud being made with only the slightest blocking-out of light-outline and dark-mass. In (2) the light areas are layed in according to the direction of sunlight. Because all clouds are the result of sunlight upon water droplets, a cloud cannot be drawn till the direction of light and shadow is first decided upon. By imagining the three-dimensional qualities of your cloud you may devise overhanging "shelves", puffs and prominences simply by using white, then shading subtly beneath with dark values. In (3) you see the effects of working **beneath** and **to the rear** with your shading; the cloud ceases to be flat, but becomes a puff standing out from the paper. Finally in (4) you see the cloud finished more, with occasional lines drawn in to simulate billowing layers. By pushing in the dark sky (blue paint, if you are working in oils) you may get a crisp yet ragged outline. Artistic license allows you to cut into the dark portion with lighter sky and to cut into the light upper cloud with darker sky.

Always as you work, a squint of the eyes will cause any "sore-thumb" or poorly done cloud part to jump into prominence so it may be immediately corrected. This habit enables you to map in cloudshapes that you did not have in mind at all but which have been suggested by quick or accidental strokes. Because you have not outlined your cloud you may build it up at will, or tear down parts that offend; the whole effect becomes clean, fresh, moving and not static.

By using gray paper with a white pastel for lighted area, soft charcoal for shaded area and a "stump" or rubbing instrument to smooth out the masses, you may learn much by making countless rough thumbnail cloud sketches such as will be seen on the following page. The darker the paper used, the more startling the three dimensional effect. And all you need is to do a few good cloudshapes to give you required confidence.

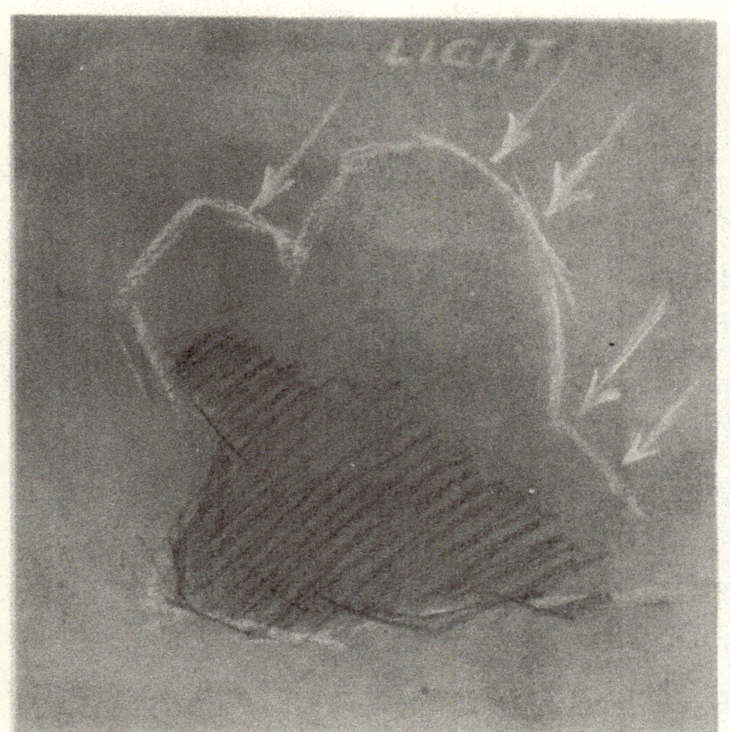

1. LEAST AMOUNT OF OUTLINE — DECISION REGARDING SOURCE OF LIGHT. DO SHADED AREA WITH DARK PENCIL OR PAINT.

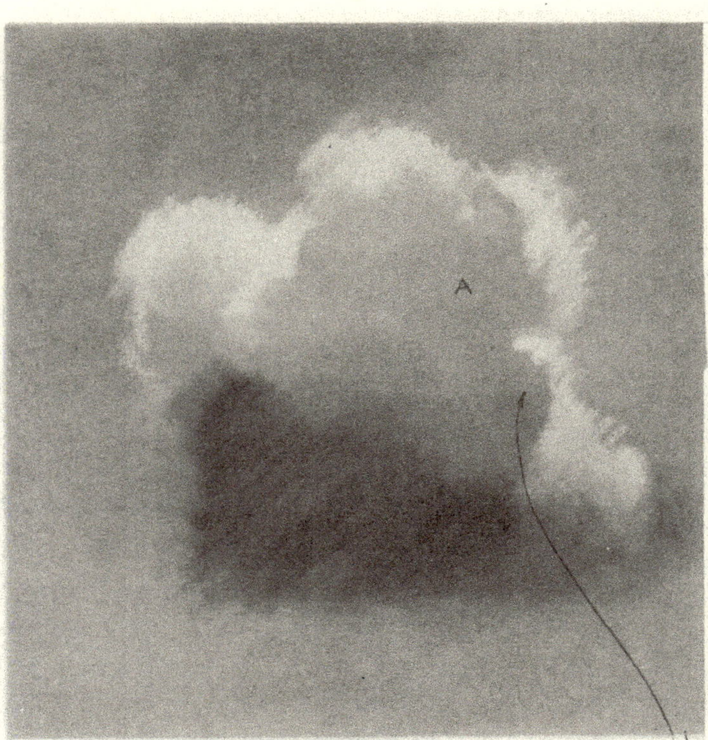

2. BRUSHING IN LIGHT AREAS, USING THEM TO "ENCASE" DARK SHADED PORTIONS.(A) THREE-DIMENSIONAL EFFECT EVOLVES.

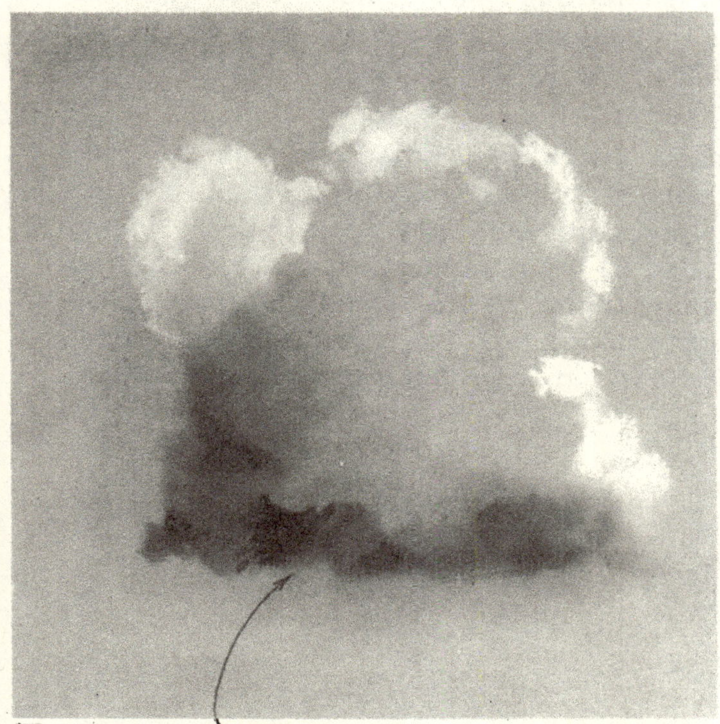

3. WORKING UNDERNEATH CLOUD WITH DARK SHADING. GENERAL SHAPING UP OF CLOUD USING MASSES INSTEAD OF OUTLINES

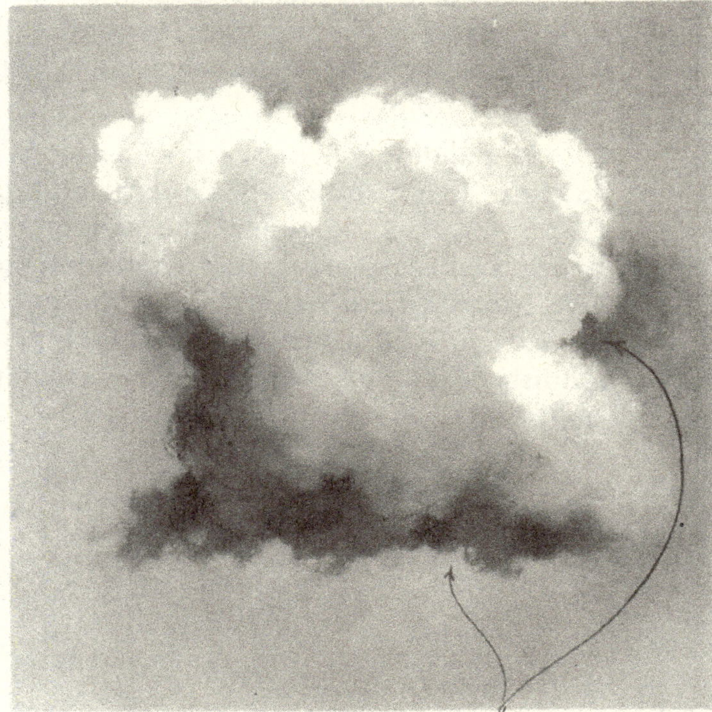

4. CUTTING IN WITH SKY TO GIVE A CRISP YET RAGGED OUTLINE. SUBTLE "BILLOW LINES" TO GIVE CLOUD A BURSTING ACTION.

CLOUD MOODS AND SHADOWS

Ordinarily, intense sunlight (which defines all cloudform against the blue of the sky) causes each billow to be highlighted and outlined by light. On rare occasions however, when a weather curtain of darkness obscures the sun, the clouds below will have a photographic-negative effect, with dark values where the light values should be. Notice the black outlines in the photograph on the opposite page (three arrows) where light outlines would normally be. Then look at the photographic-negative effect in the cloud at the center-background; observe there the light where shadows would usually be seen, giving appearance of a light glowing from within.

This reverse effect produces a dramatic sky, sombre and awe-inspiring. Viewed from below, the same trick may be done to illustrate any threatening sky, showing dark lumps in the above cloud-ceiling, with lights where the shadows should be. The opposite photograph might well contain a plane in the center, to illustrate a story on hurricanes or rough weather flying.

Below you may see sketches showing the two techniques, first the usual pleasant light-outlined cloud (on the left), then the angry or sullen interpretation (on the right) with dark outlines and inner lights.

You may see this reverse effect when a line-squall or summer thunderstorm approaches, but the same thing (exaggerated) occurs in any great oil fire. Perhaps you will remember news-shots of some oil fire showing the dark billows with lights flickering from within.

In painting an angry sky in colors, black should be avoided and something like Payne's Gray substituted. Greens, blue-greens and purples may be brushed into dark clouds for they do reflect the sea or the landscape that they hover above. Distant clouds such as those in the center-background of the opposite picture should be reddish (possibly Geranium Lake with Pale Yellow to tint the cloud-white) to portray distance. You will notice that threatening thunderheads just over the horizon are deep reddish or orange, with only the sunlit portions showing, the rest of the cloud-body melting into the distant shades.

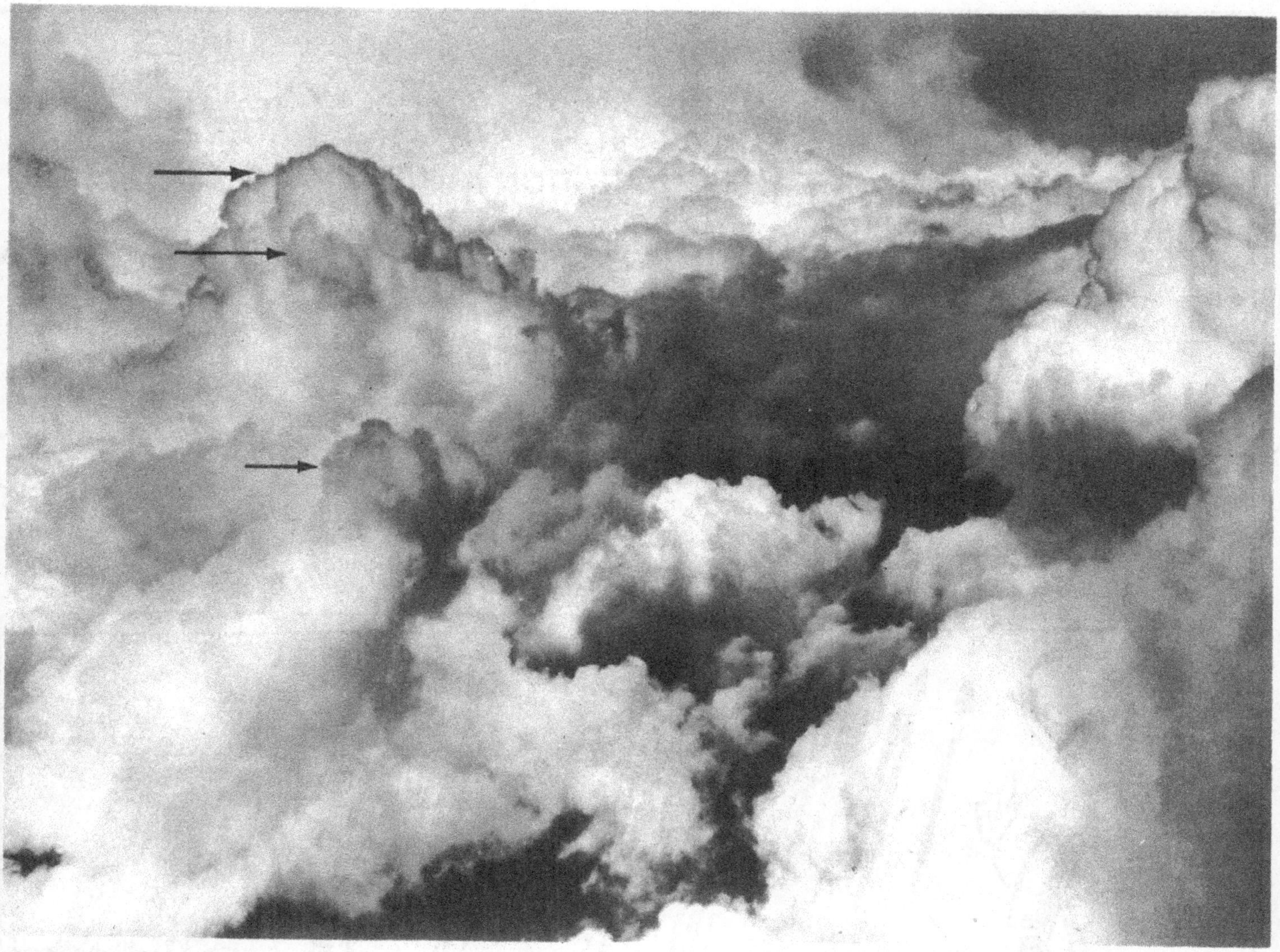

ABOVE, YOU SEE A PHOTO OF AN ANGRY CLOUDSCAPE. NOTICE THE MANY DARK-OUTLINED CONTOURS, GIVING THE BOILING APPEARANCE.

BELOW YOU SEE A CLOUDSHAPE WITH LIGHT OUTLINES. AND THE SAME SHAPE TREATED WITH "ANGRY" DARK OUTLINES.

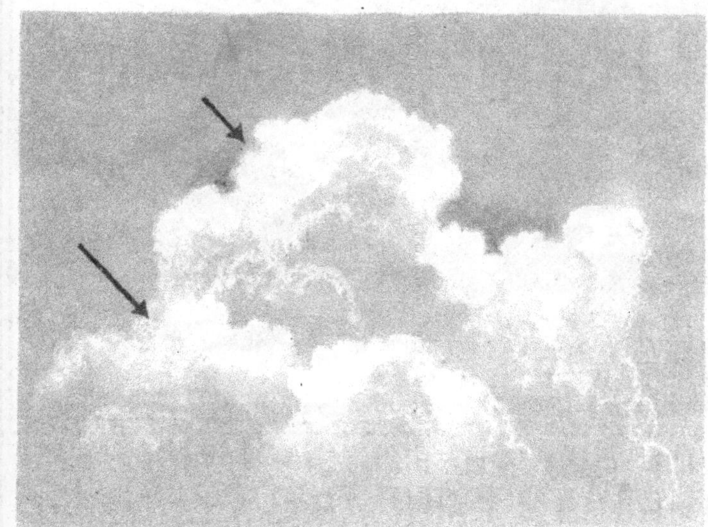

LIGHT COMES FROM ABOVE HERE

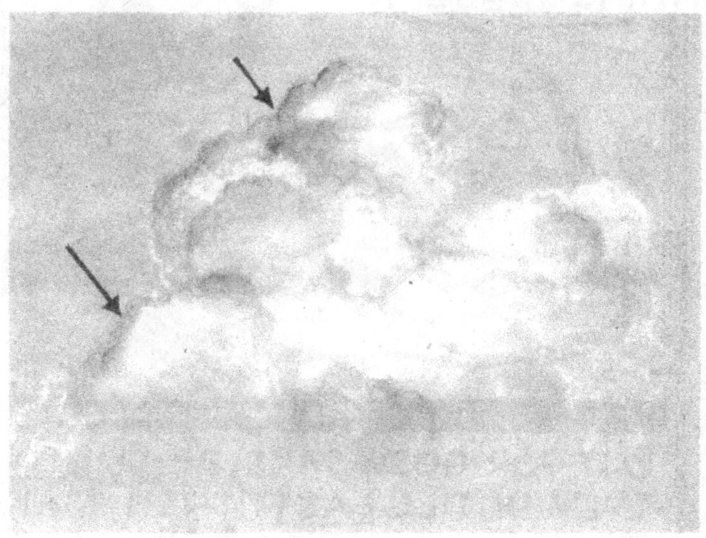

LIGHT COMES FROM "WITHIN".

YOU · WILL · OFTEN · HEAR · SUNBEAMS · *and* · SHADOW-SHAFTS REFERRED · TO · AS "THE · SUN · DRAWING · WATER". ACTUALLY, THIS IS · AN · AREA · WHERE · THE · SUN · IS · **NOT** DRAWING · WATER! ALL · SUNLIGHT · DRAWS · WATER (EVAPORATION) BUT · WHERE · CLOUDS BLOT · OUT · THE · SUNLIGHT, SHADOW-SHAFTS · OCCUR.

KEEP · SHADOW · SHAFTS PARALLEL · IF · SUN · IS OVERHEAD

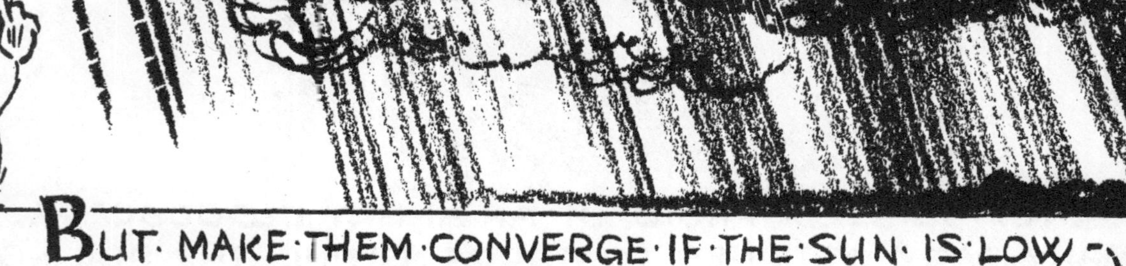

BUT · MAKE · THEM · CONVERGE · IF · THE · SUN · IS · LOW

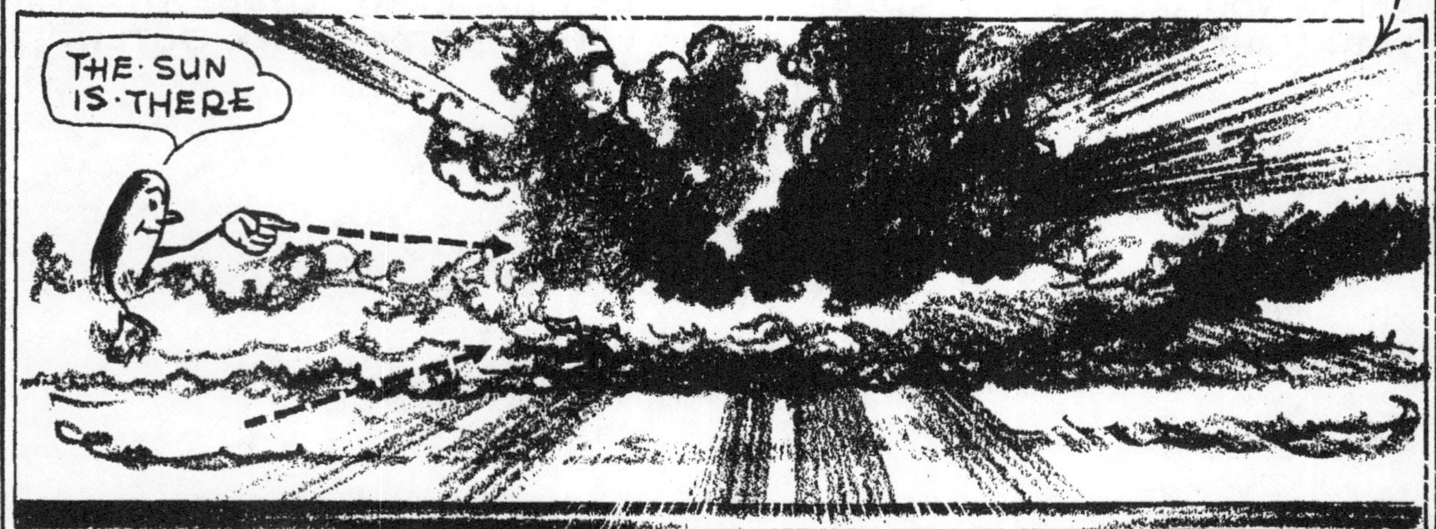

BUT · FOR · GOSH · SAKE, BE · SUBTLE · WITH · SKY · SHADOWS.. **DON'T** PUT THEM · IN · TILL · LAST; THEN · MAKE · THEM · SO · FAINT · THAT · SQUINTING THE · EYES · MAKES · THEM · DISAPPEAR. THEY · ALMOST **AIN'T**!

AN AIRPLANE MAY BE ADDED TO A CLOUDSCAPE TO INDICATE THE IMMENSITY OF CLOUD MASSES *providing the plane is* **SMALL**.

SEE HOW SMALL THIS CLOUD LOOKS

WHILE THIS CLOUD IS MOUNTAINOUS!

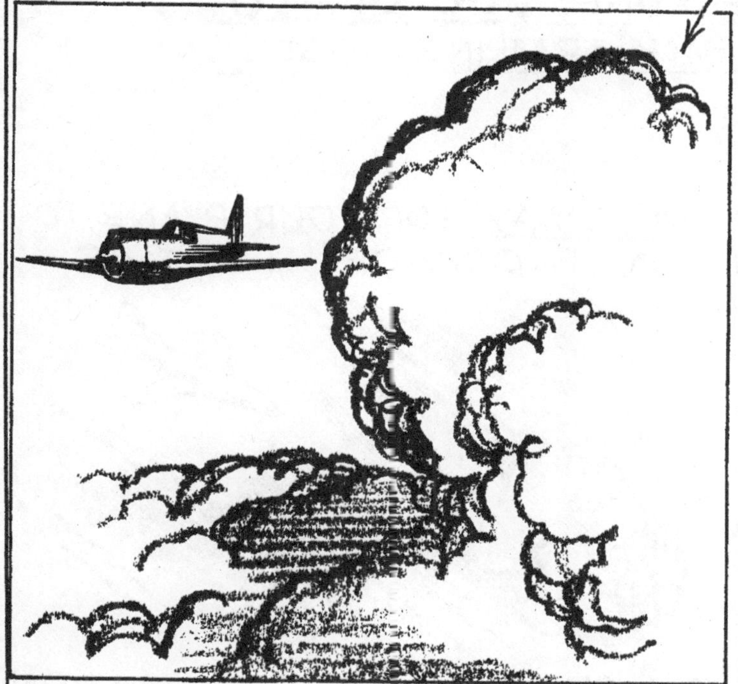

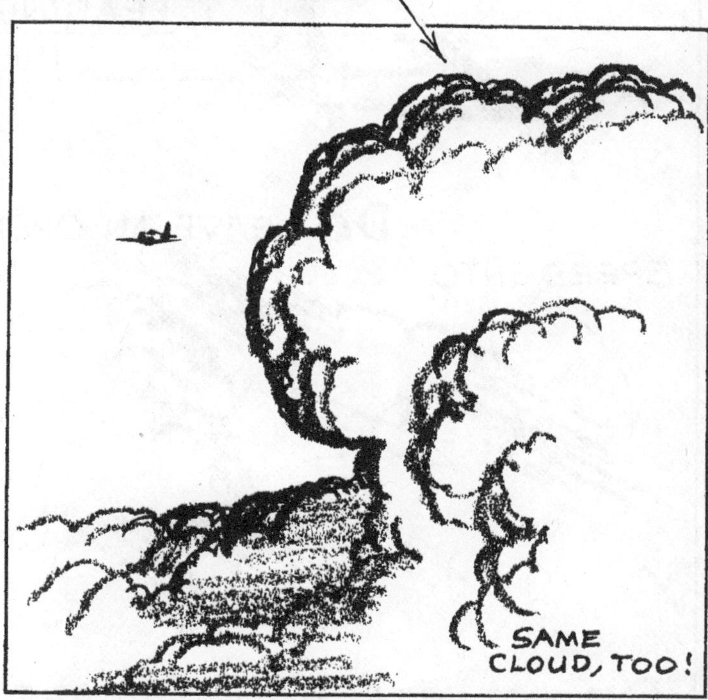

..AND TO GIVE *the* PLANE MOVEMENT, PUT *the* **MASS** BEHIND IT TO "PUSH" FORWARD. FOR INSTANCE, BELOW YOU SEE AN OBJECT WHICH APPEARS TO BE FLYING TO THE LEFT......BY

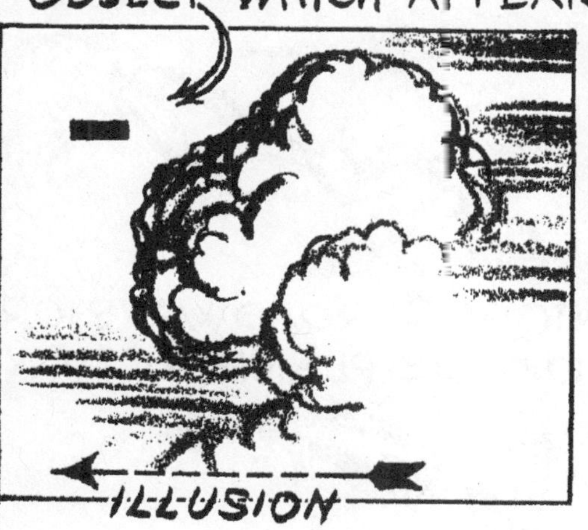

MAKING IT A PLANE FLYING TOWARD THE CLOUD MASS THE PLANE GIVES THE IMPRESSION OF FLYING BACKWARDS!

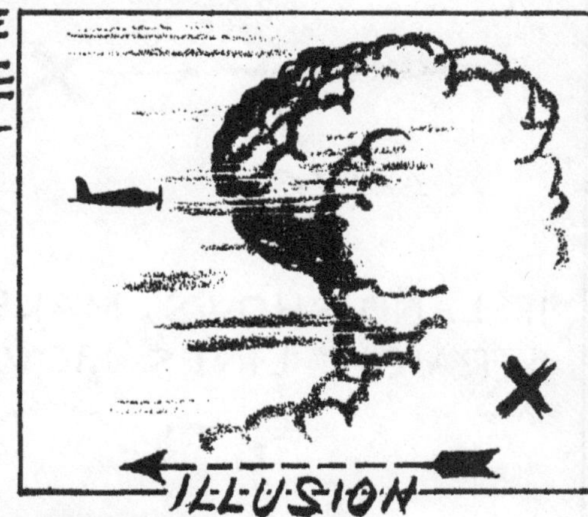

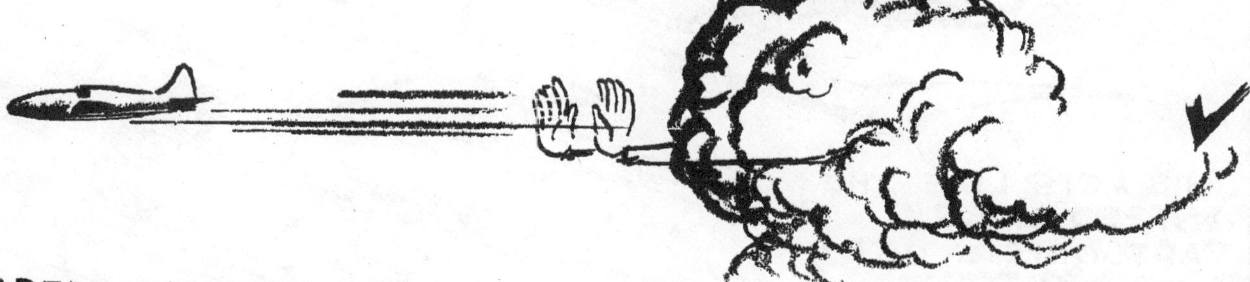

SO

REMEMBER – MAKE YOUR CLOUD MASS PUSH YOUR PLANE AHEAD.

—AND ON THE SUBJECT OF AIRPLANE ACTION, SHOULD YOUR PICTURE BE ONE OF A <u>PLANE</u> RATHER THAN ONE OF <u>CLOUDS</u>, THERE A FEW "TRICKS·OF·MOVEMENT" WORTH REMEMBERING. FOR EXAMPLE, **DO** MAKE SHARP, HEAVY LEADING EDGES, **DO** **SHADE OFF** THE BACK "TRAILING EDGES"

DO LEAVE AN OPEN "ROADWAY" FOR YOUR PLANE TO SPEED INTO ..... NOT A "BLOCKADE" LIKE THIS

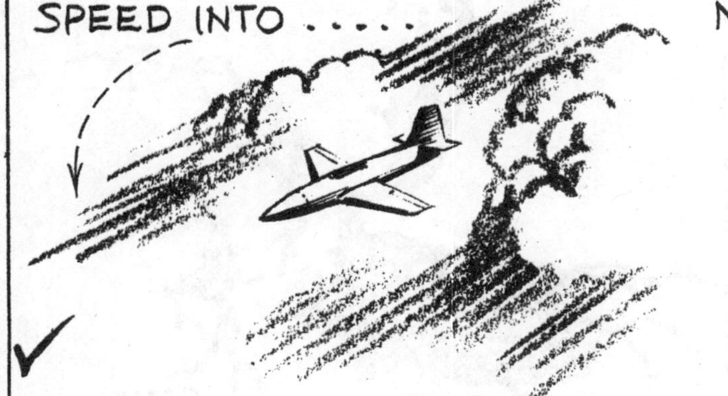

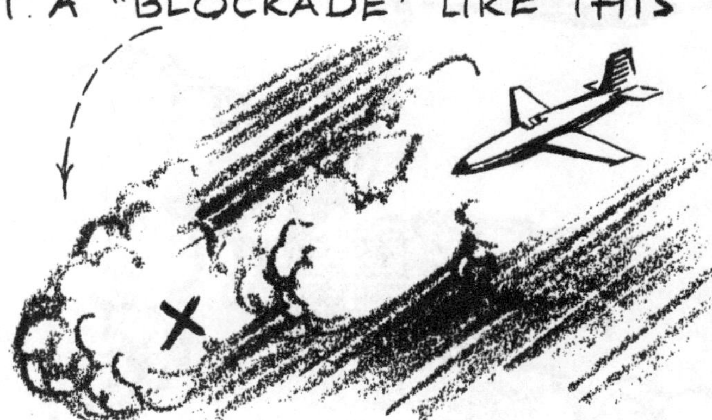

DO NOT "ATTACH" YOUR PLANE TO A CLOUD *and* ARREST ACTION. BUT LIFT IT OFF .. MAKE IT **FLY**!

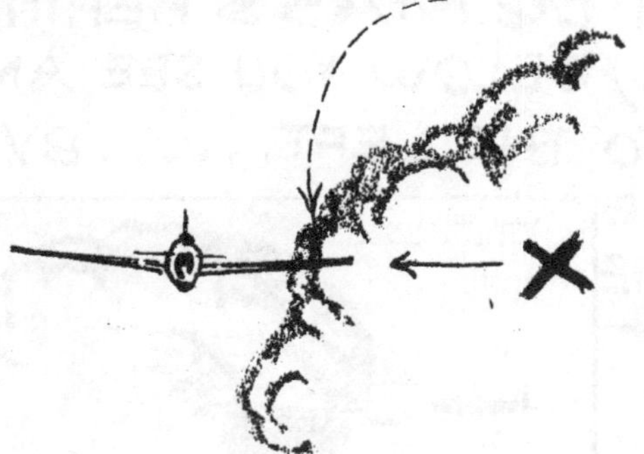

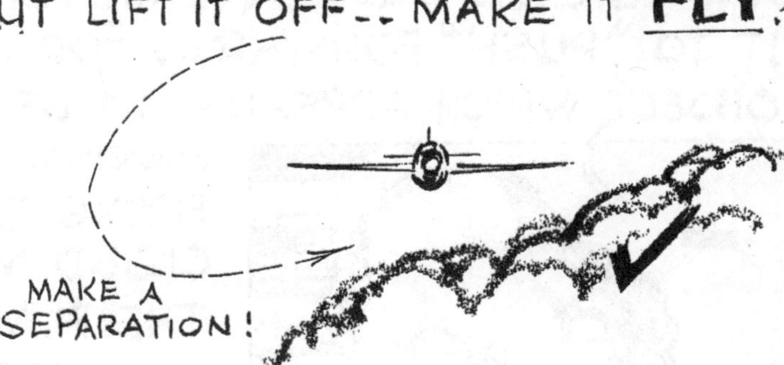

IF·LAND·SHOWS, MAKE·ALL·IMPORTANT·CONTOURS, ROADWAYS·OR STRAIGHT·LINES "MOVE" IN·THE·DIRECTION·OF·THE·PLANE·ACTION

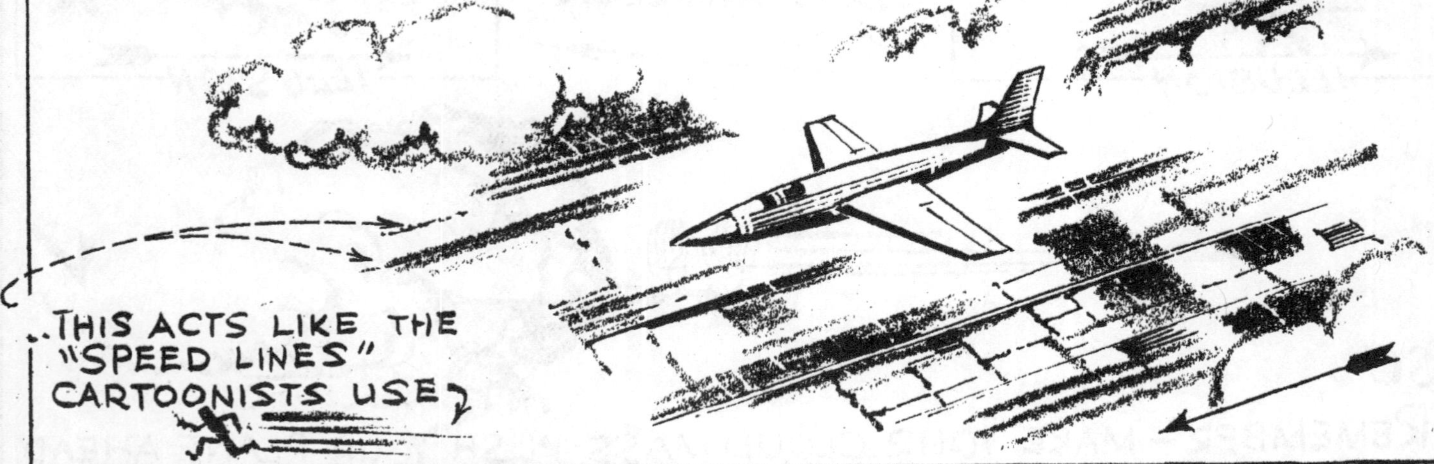

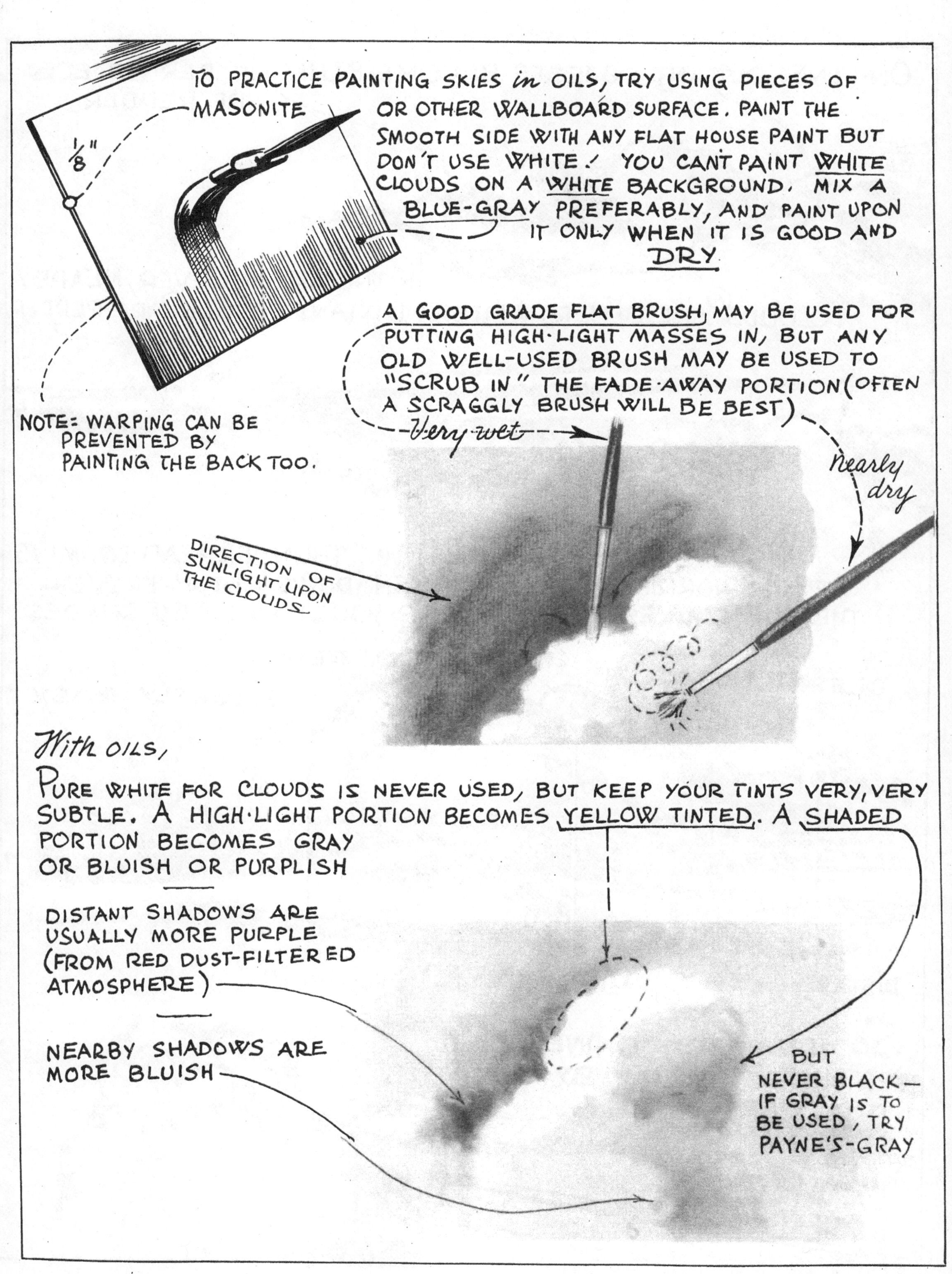

TO PRACTICE PAINTING SKIES *in* OILS, TRY USING PIECES OF MASONITE OR OTHER WALLBOARD SURFACE. PAINT THE SMOOTH SIDE WITH ANY FLAT HOUSE PAINT BUT DON'T USE WHITE! YOU CAN'T PAINT WHITE CLOUDS ON A WHITE BACKGROUND. MIX A BLUE-GRAY PREFERABLY, AND PAINT UPON IT ONLY WHEN IT IS GOOD AND DRY.
1/8"
NOTE: WARPING CAN BE PREVENTED BY PAINTING THE BACK TOO.
A GOOD GRADE FLAT BRUSH MAY BE USED FOR PUTTING HIGH-LIGHT MASSES IN, BUT ANY OLD WELL-USED BRUSH MAY BE USED TO "SCRUB IN" THE FADE-AWAY PORTION (OFTEN A SCRAGGLY BRUSH WILL BE BEST)
Very wet
Nearly dry
DIRECTION OF SUNLIGHT UPON THE CLOUDS
With OILS,
PURE WHITE FOR CLOUDS IS NEVER USED, BUT KEEP YOUR TINTS VERY, VERY SUBTLE. A HIGH-LIGHT PORTION BECOMES YELLOW TINTED. A SHADED PORTION BECOMES GRAY OR BLUISH OR PURPLISH
DISTANT SHADOWS ARE USUALLY MORE PURPLE (FROM RED DUST-FILTERED ATMOSPHERE)
NEARBY SHADOWS ARE MORE BLUISH
BUT NEVER BLACK— IF GRAY IS TO BE USED, TRY PAYNE'S-GRAY

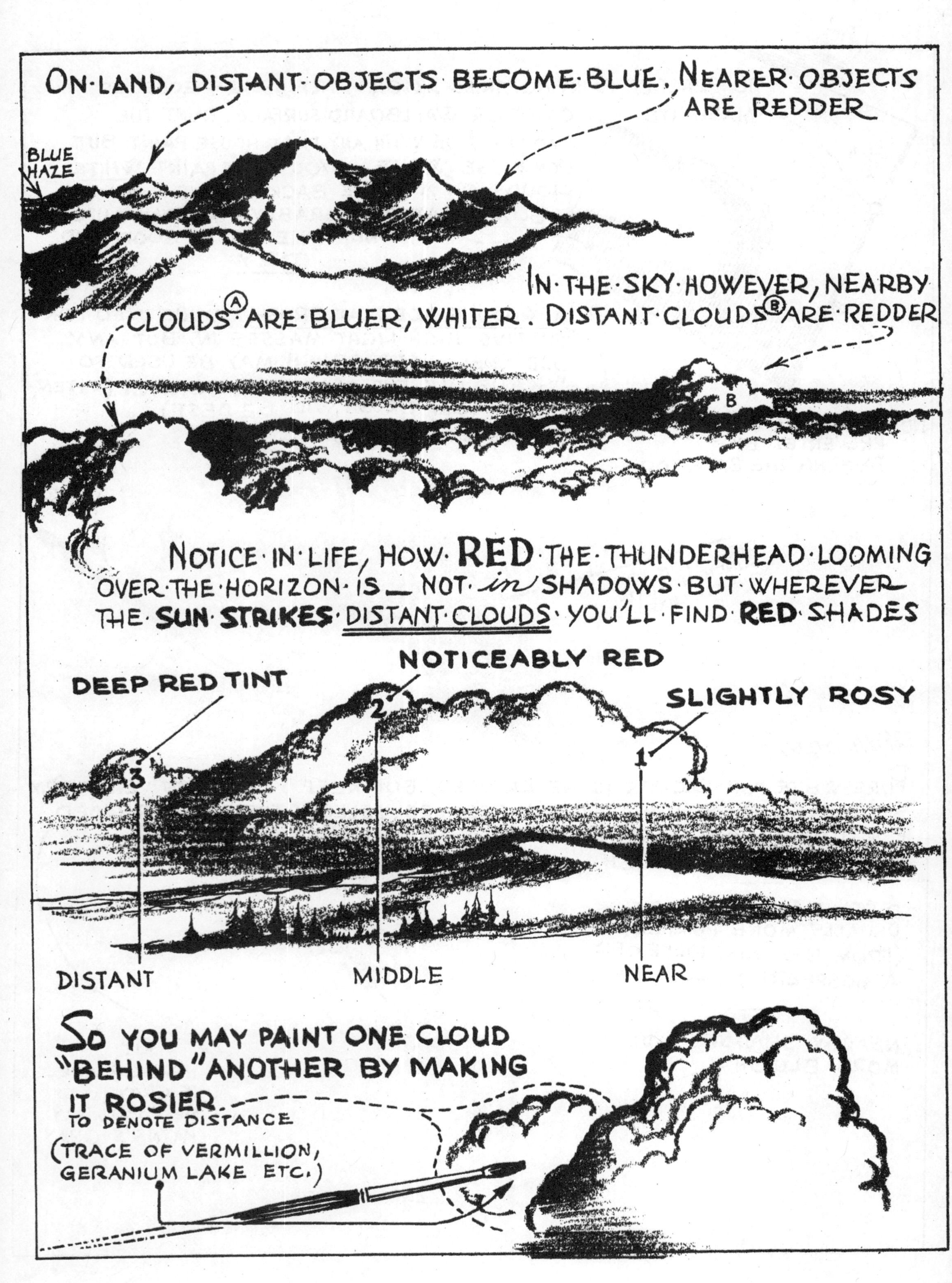
ON·LAND, DISTANT·OBJECTS·BECOME·BLUE. NEARER·OBJECTS ARE REDDER
BLUE HAZE
IN·THE·SKY·HOWEVER, NEARBY CLOUDS(A)·ARE·BLUER, WHITER. DISTANT·CLOUDS(B)·ARE·REDDER
B
NOTICE·IN·LIFE, HOW·RED·THE·THUNDERHEAD·LOOMING OVER·THE·HORIZON·IS — NOT·in·SHADOWS·BUT·WHEREVER THE·SUN·STRIKES·DISTANT·CLOUDS·YOU'LL·FIND·RED·SHADES
NOTICEABLY RED
DEEP RED TINT
SLIGHTLY ROSY
2
3
1
DISTANT
MIDDLE
NEAR
SO YOU MAY PAINT ONE CLOUD "BEHIND" ANOTHER BY MAKING IT ROSIER.
TO DENOTE DISTANCE
(TRACE OF VERMILLION, GERANIUM LAKE ETC.)

SKY *and* EARTH ALWAYS MATCH *in* MOOD *and* VERY OFTEN *in* COLORING: SENSING THIS *and* PUTTING IT *on* CANVAS *is a* SUBTLE, DELICATE BIT OF WORK, OFTEN DONE *as a* LAST TOUCH *and with a* NEARLY DRY BRUSH

JUST AS THE SKY RELECTS UPON WATER, THE SEA CAN REFLECT AGAINST LOW HANGING CLOUDS. THEREFORE WHEN PUTTING DARK UNDER-SHADE ON CLOUDS, DO USE A BIT OF THE SHADE USED *on the* SEASCAPE *or* LANDSCAPE BELOW

GREEN GRAY

PINK-GRAY

GREEN GRAY

PINK-GRAY

IN FACT, YOU MAY RUB SEA-COLOR DIRECTLY FROM THE HORIZON, INTO THE SKY — TO MAKE THE SEA-HORIZON LESS DISTINCT

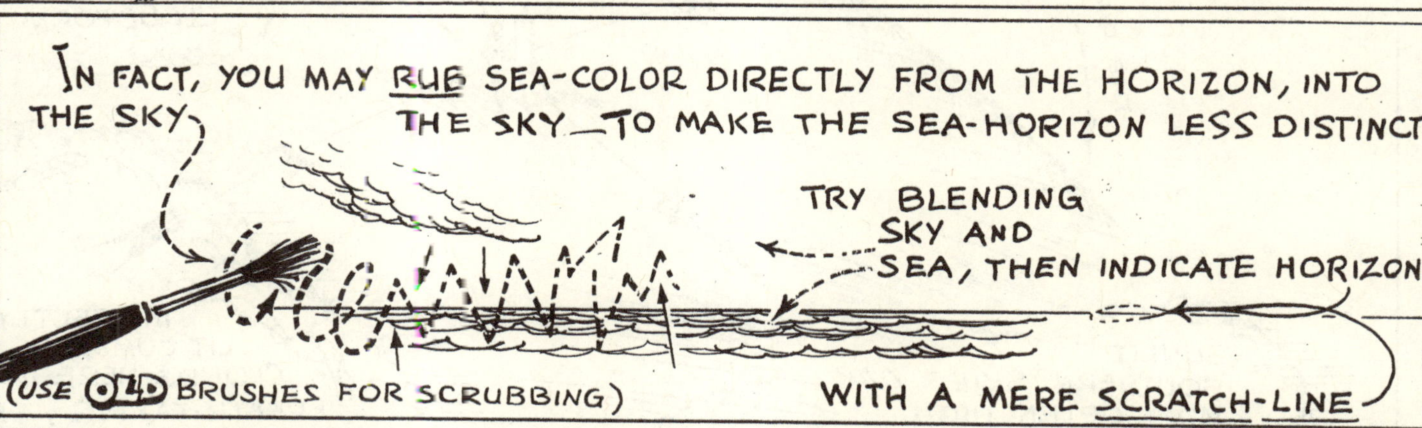

JUST AS DISTANT CLOUDS BECOME REDDISH *with* DISTANCE, *the* SKY ITSELF (MOSTLY *when the* SUN IS LOW) MAY BECOME RED *or* PURPLE. DO NOTE HOW HORIZON-HAZE IS DEEP *and* OF PURPLE SHADE, OFTEN LOOKING EXACTLY LIKE A DISTANT MOUNTAIN

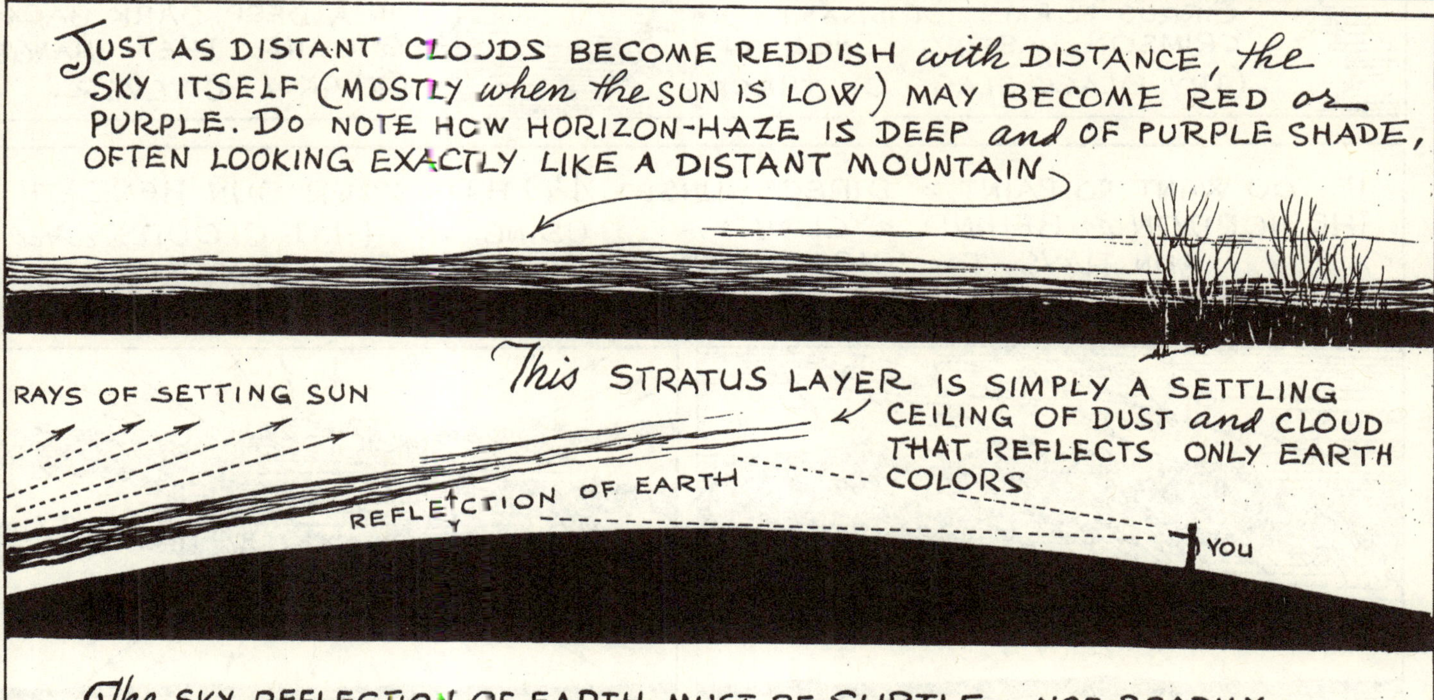

The SKY REFLECTION OF EARTH MUST BE SUBTLE — NOT READILY NOTICEABLE.... MUDDYING *the* SKY TAKES AWAY ITS TRANSPARANCY. *The* REFLECTION EFFECT IS BEST SCRUBBED IN AFTER THE PICTURE IS NEARLY DRY.

SUNSETS

ARE VARIED *in* POSITION *and* MOOD. LOOKING DIRECTLY AT *the* SUNSET *is the* MOST DIFFICULT, OFTEN THE LEAST EFFECTIVE VIEW. PAINTING THE NAKED SUN IS LIKE PAINTING *a* LIT ELECTRIC LIGHT BULB.

RATHER PUT YOUR SUN BEHIND A CLOUD *and* FEATURE SUN RAYS, OR SHOW YOUR SUNSET *as* INDIRECT LIGHTING

SUNRISE BY THE WAY, IS IDENTICAL TO SUNSET EXCEPT FOR THE FREQUENT PRESENCE OF MISTS.

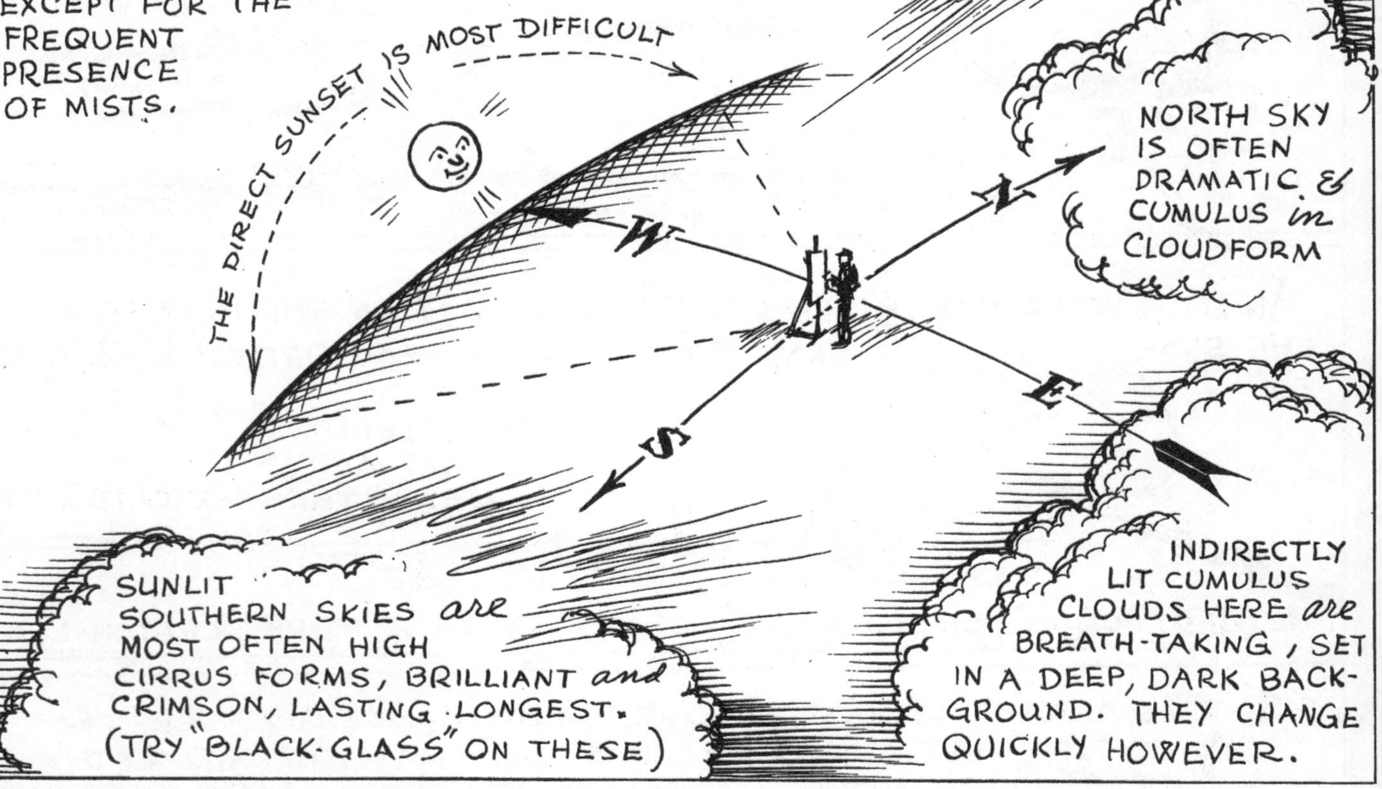

CIRRUS, CRIMSON TO PURPLE

THE DIRECT SUNSET IS MOST DIFFICULT

NORTH SKY IS OFTEN DRAMATIC & CUMULUS *in* CLOUDFORM

W

N

S

E

SUNLIT SOUTHERN SKIES *are* MOST OFTEN HIGH CIRRUS FORMS, BRILLIANT *and* CRIMSON, LASTING LONGEST. (TRY "BLACK-GLASS" ON THESE)

INDIRECTLY LIT CUMULUS CLOUDS HERE *are* BREATH-TAKING, SET IN A DEEP, DARK BACKGROUND. THEY CHANGE QUICKLY HOWEVER.

IF YOU WANT TO PAINT *a* DIRECT SUNSET, DO HIDE YOUR SUN BENEATH THE HORIZON *or* BEHIND *a* CLOUD, USING HIGH-LIT CLOUDS *and* SUN RAYS TO SHOW WHERE THE SUN IS SITUATED.

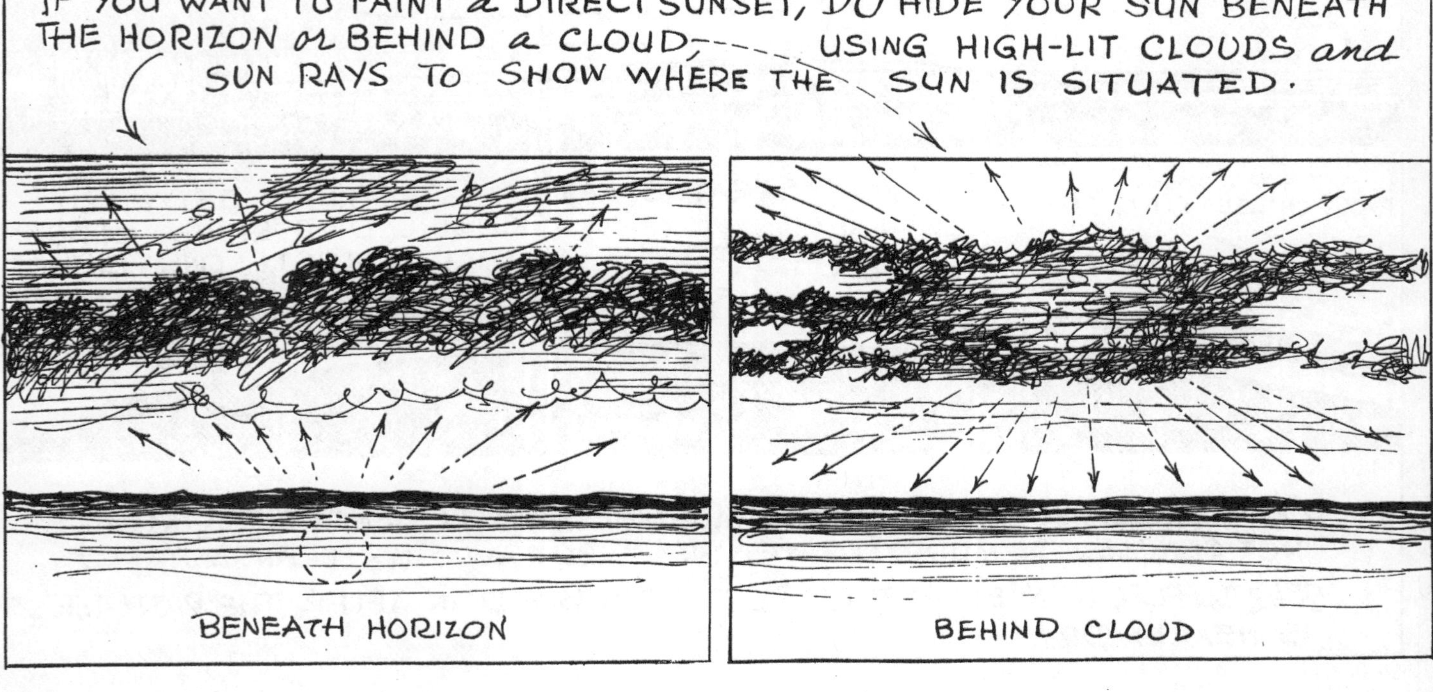

BENEATH HORIZON

BEHIND CLOUD

THE CLOUD ARTIST'S PALETTE IS SELDOM *a* NEAT ONE. YOU WILL FIND YOURSELF "INVENTING" COLORS *and* MIXING SHADES BOTH ON YOUR PALETTE *and* ON YOUR ACTUAL CANVAS, *as* YOU WORK. DONT TRY TO BE TOO NEAT... MIX *and* APPLY PAINT BOLDLY.

HERE WE SEE *a* VERY SIMPLE PALETTE. NOTICE *the* LARGE AMOUNT OF WHITE.

BECAUSE OF *the* MUCH RUBBING *and* SCRUBBING *with a* PARTLY DRY BRUSH. **RAGS** *are an* IMPORTANT PART OF *the* CLOUD ARTIST'S EQUIPMENT

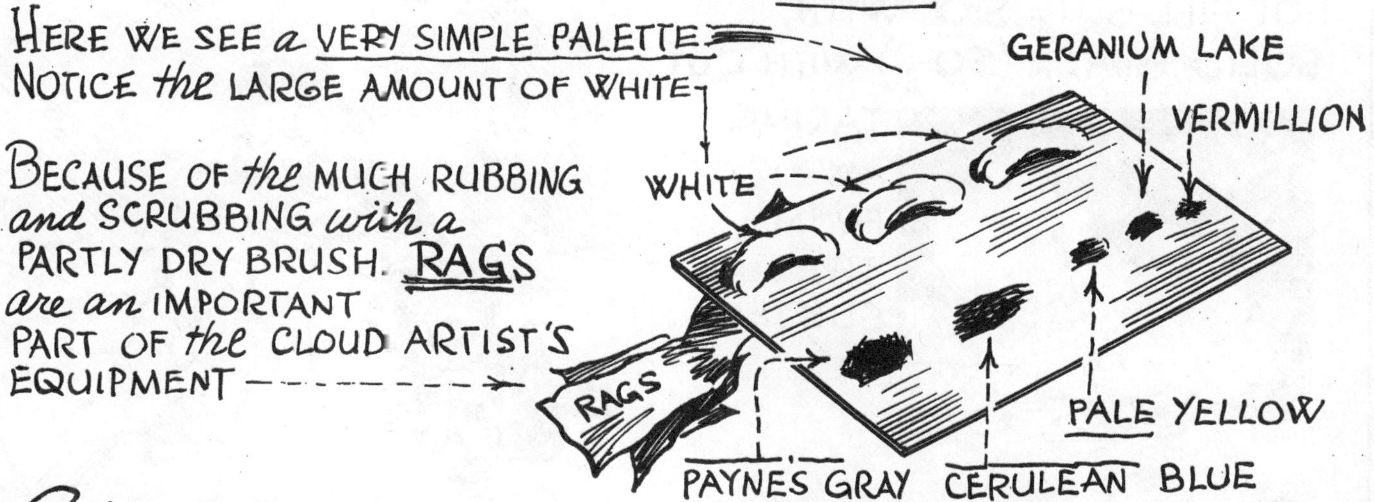

Your CLOUDSCAPE PALETTE WILL PROBABLY BE SO MESSY THAT YOU WILL PREFER USING *an* OLD PIECE OF MASONITE WALL BOARD, DESTROYING *the* SAME WHEN FINISHED WITH IT.

DO

AVOID USING BLACK. TO SIMULATE BLACK, USE *a* VERY DARK BLUE *with* **ALIZARIN**. ALSO AVOID REDDISH *or* DEEP YELLOWS.. USE LEMON OR PALE YELLOWS. A TOUCH *of* YELLOW *will* BRIGHTEN *a* BLUE SKY.

NEVER PAINT SKIES *at an* ANGLE.. IT DISTORTS *the* PERSPECTIVE. DO USE *an* EASEL WHERE YOU MAY WALK A DISTANCE AWAY *to* VIEW DEFECTS *and to* "FEEL" *the* AERIAL DISTANCES.

IT WILL HELP YOU TO FEEL CLOUDSHAPES BETTER, IF YOU PAINT "UP TO" THE CLOUD BOTTOMS AND PAINT "DOWN TO" THE CLOUD TOPS. (RAISING *and* LOWERING YOUR EASEL).

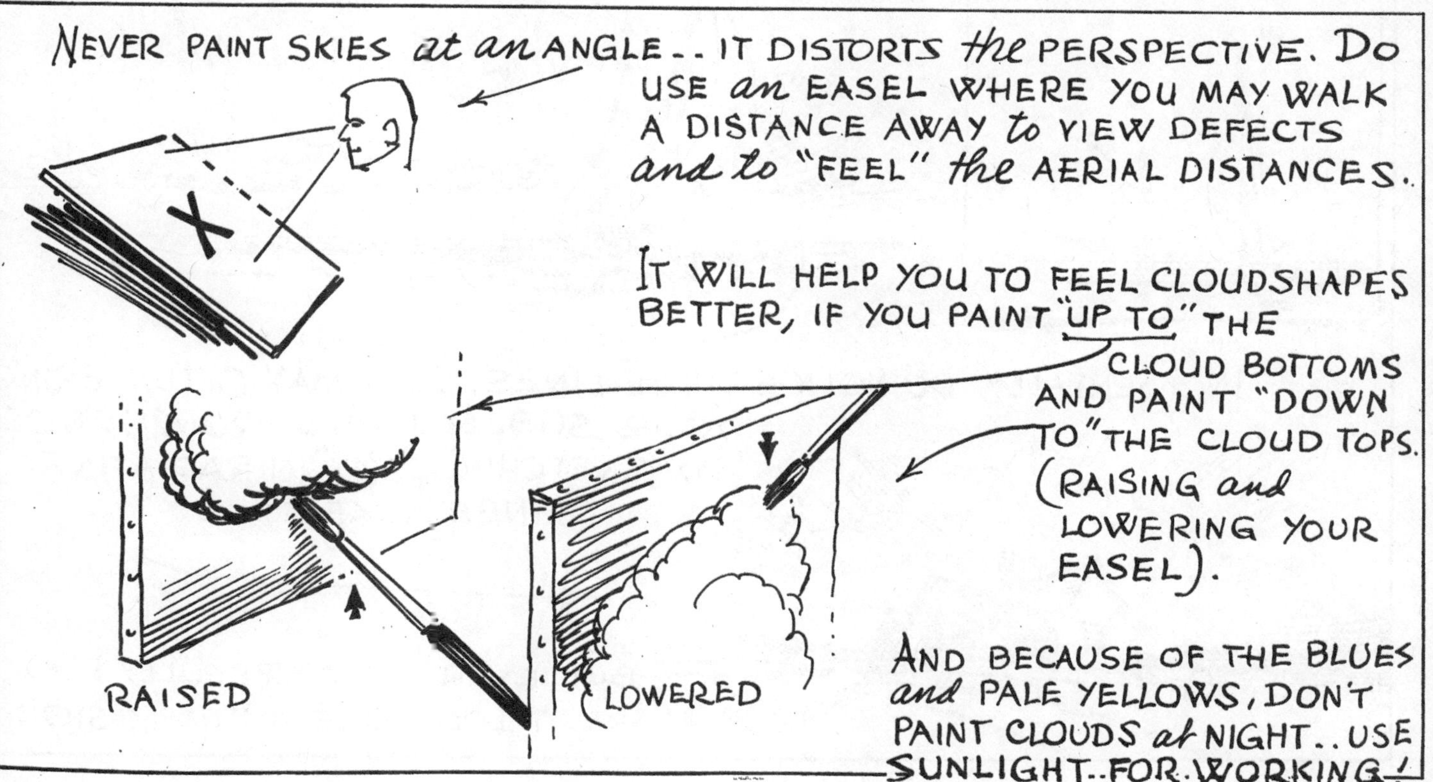

AND BECAUSE OF THE BLUES *and* PALE YELLOWS, DON'T PAINT CLOUDS *at* NIGHT.. USE SUNLIGHT..FOR WORKING!

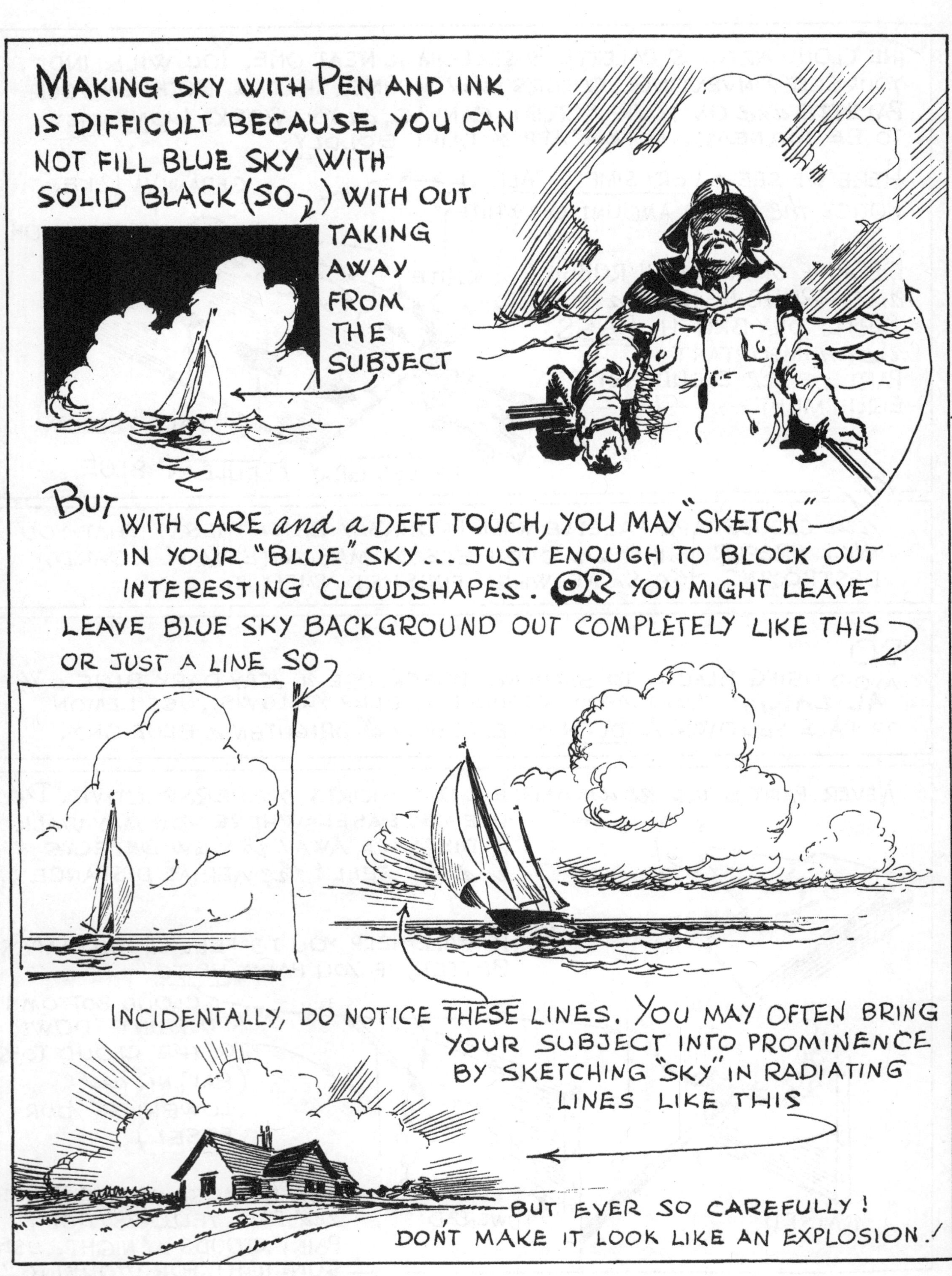
MAKING SKY WITH PEN AND INK IS DIFFICULT BECAUSE YOU CAN NOT FILL BLUE SKY WITH SOLID BLACK (SO) WITH OUT TAKING AWAY FROM THE SUBJECT
BUT WITH CARE and a DEFT TOUCH, YOU MAY "SKETCH" IN YOUR "BLUE" SKY... JUST ENOUGH TO BLOCK OUT INTERESTING CLOUDSHAPES. OR YOU MIGHT LEAVE LEAVE BLUE SKY BACKGROUND OUT COMPLETELY LIKE THIS
OR JUST A LINE SO
INCIDENTALLY, DO NOTICE THESE LINES. YOU MAY OFTEN BRING YOUR SUBJECT INTO PROMINENCE BY SKETCHING "SKY" IN RADIATING LINES LIKE THIS
BUT EVER SO CAREFULLY! DON'T MAKE IT LOOK LIKE AN EXPLOSION!

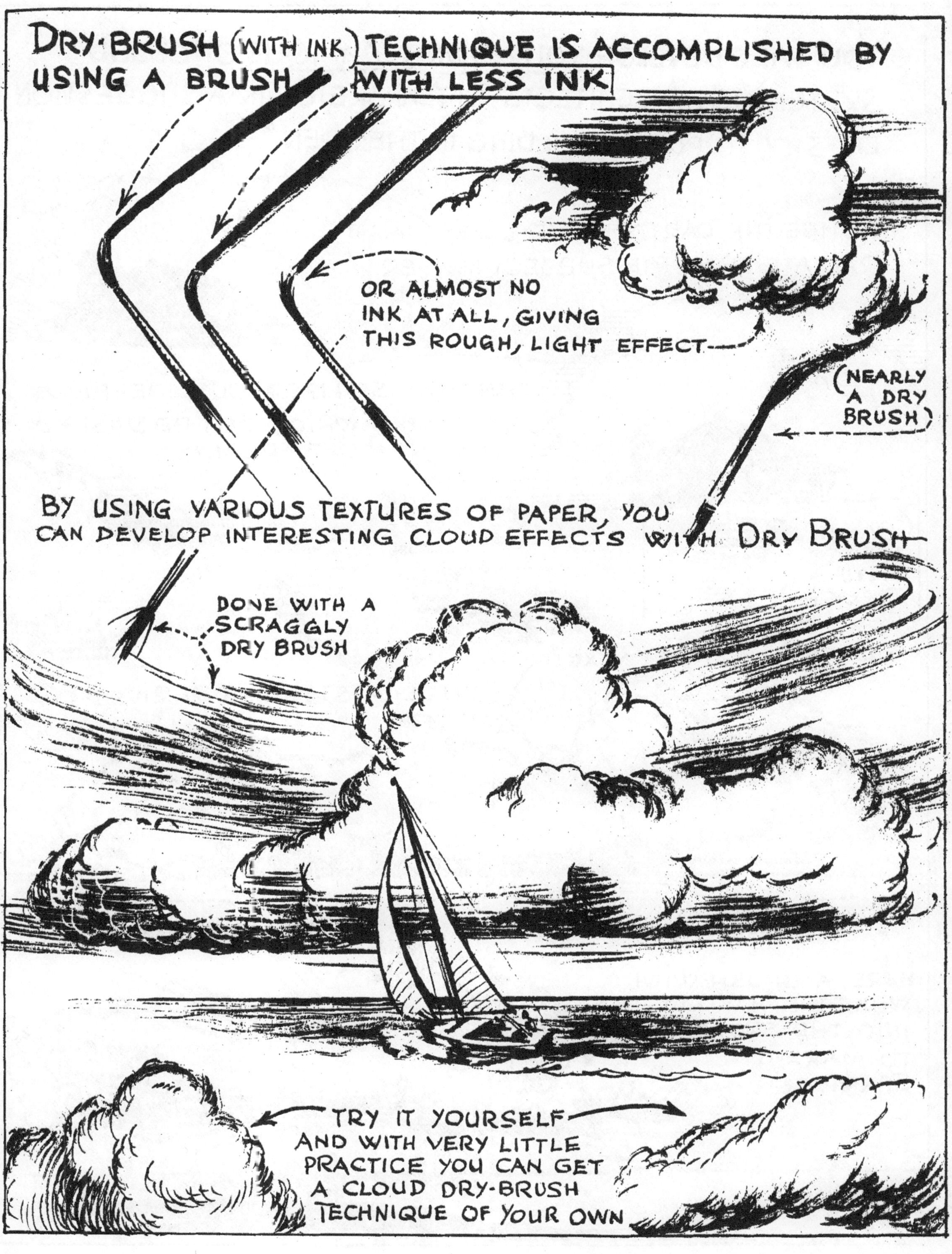
DRY·BRUSH (WITH INK) TECHNIQUE IS ACCOMPLISHED BY USING A BRUSH WITH LESS INK
OR ALMOST NO INK AT ALL, GIVING THIS ROUGH, LIGHT EFFECT
(NEARLY A DRY BRUSH)
BY USING VARIOUS TEXTURES OF PAPER, YOU CAN DEVELOP INTERESTING CLOUD EFFECTS WITH DRY BRUSH
DONE WITH A SCRAGGLY DRY BRUSH
TRY IT YOURSELF
AND WITH VERY LITTLE PRACTICE YOU CAN GET A CLOUD DRY-BRUSH TECHNIQUE OF YOUR OWN

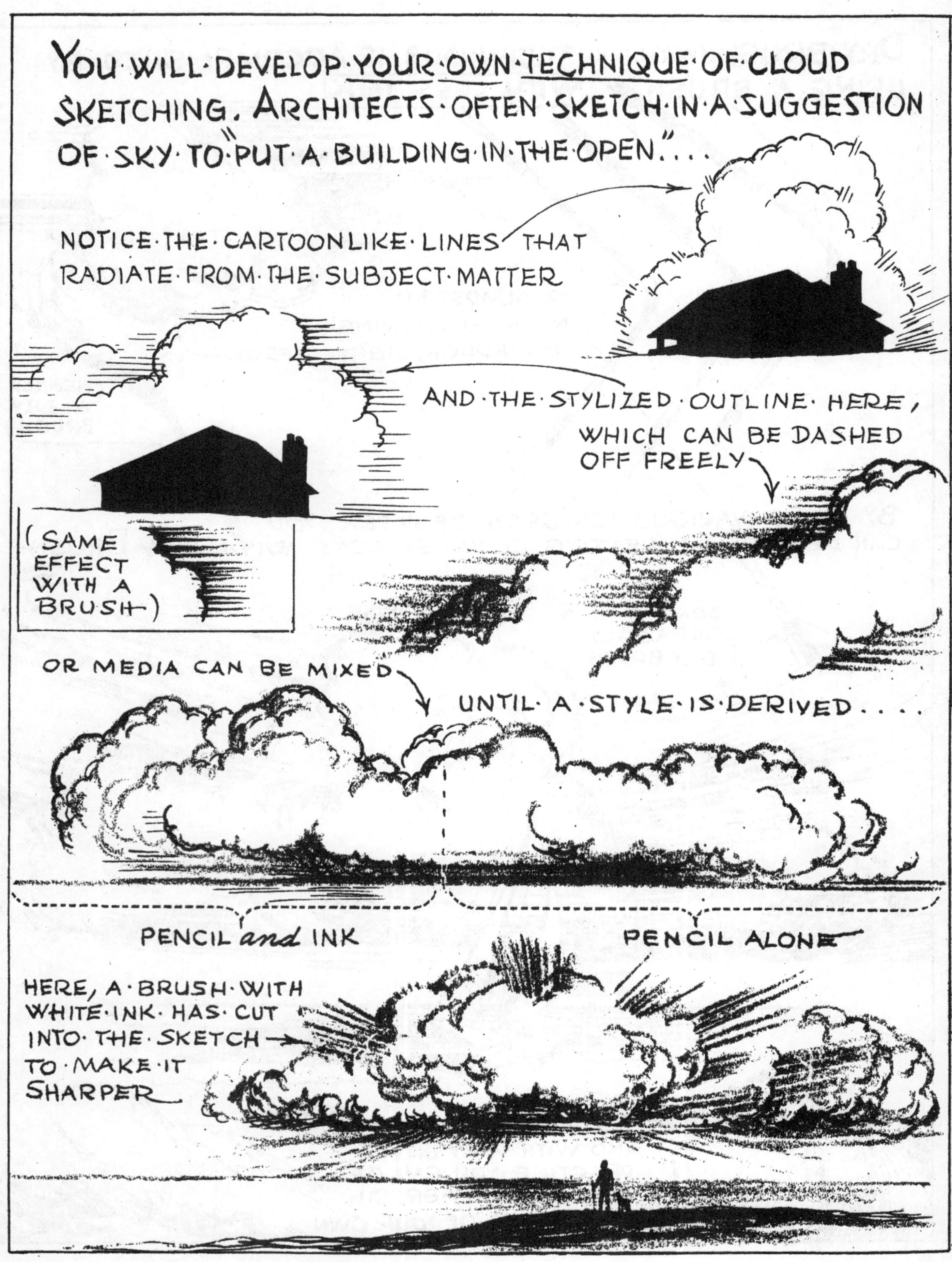
YOU·WILL·DEVELOP·YOUR·OWN·TECHNIQUE·OF·CLOUD SKETCHING. ARCHITECTS·OFTEN·SKETCH·IN·A·SUGGESTION OF·SKY·TO "PUT·A·BUILDING·IN·THE·OPEN"...
NOTICE·THE·CARTOONLIKE·LINES THAT RADIATE·FROM·THE·SUBJECT·MATTER
AND·THE·STYLIZED·OUTLINE·HERE, WHICH CAN BE DASHED OFF FREELY
(SAME EFFECT WITH A BRUSH)
OR MEDIA CAN BE MIXED
UNTIL·A·STYLE·IS·DERIVED....
PENCIL and INK
PENCIL ALONE
HERE, A·BRUSH·WITH WHITE·INK·HAS·CUT INTO·THE·SKETCH TO·MAKE·IT SHARPER

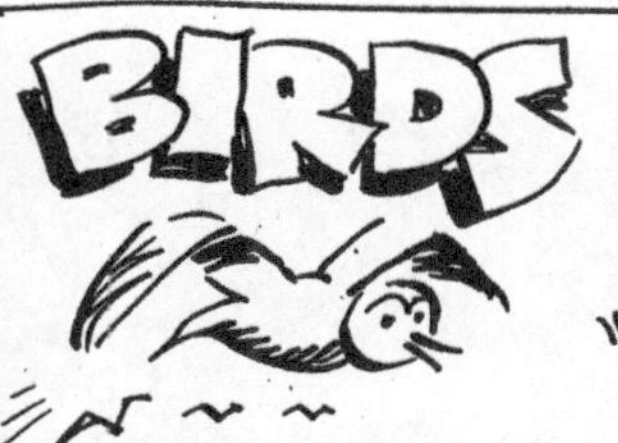

GIVE CLOUDSCAPES INTEREST, ACTION *and* REALNESS. A SEASIDE SKY *or* PRAIRIE SKY *might* APPEAR BLANK *and* LIFELESS . . . A FLIGHT *of* DUCKS *or* GEESE *added*, MIGHT "MAKE" THE PICTURE.

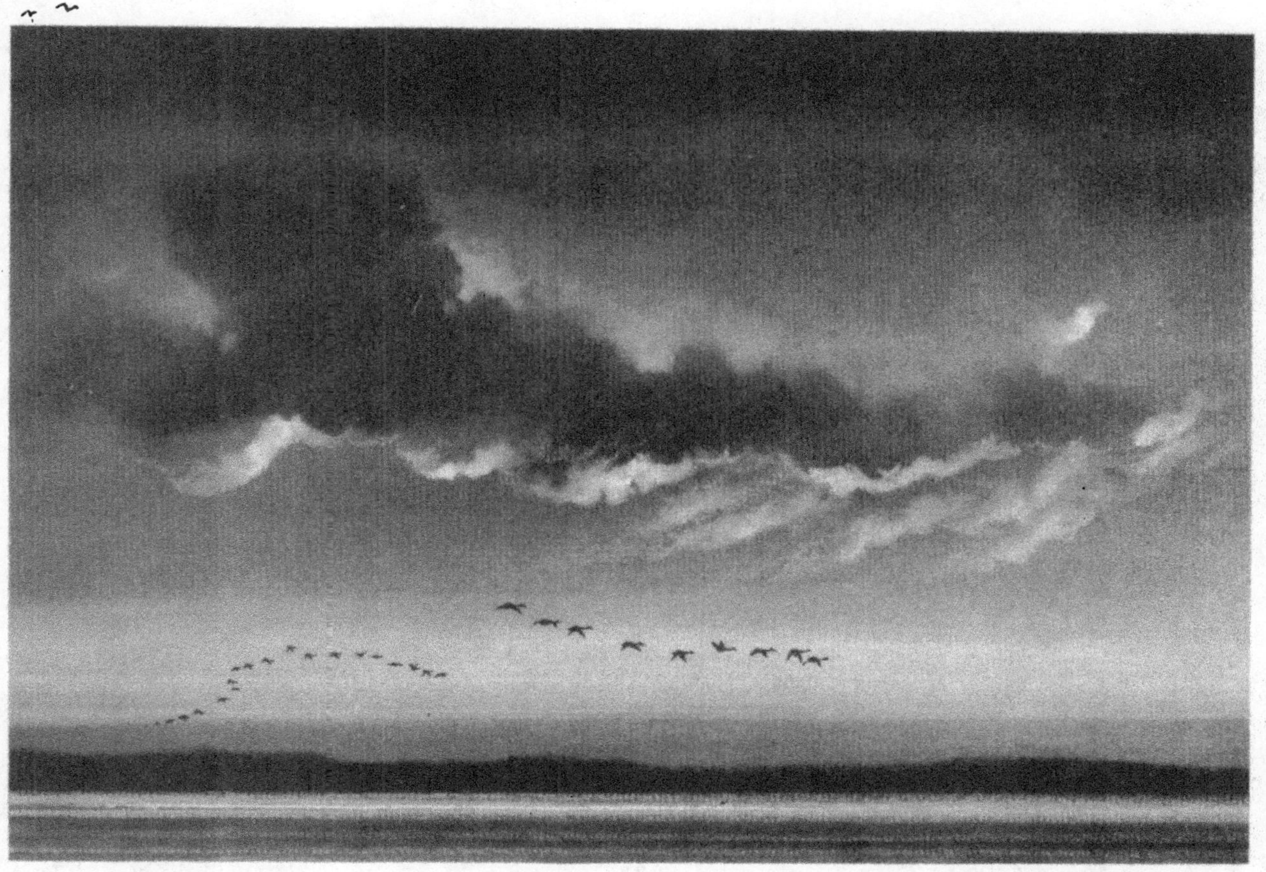

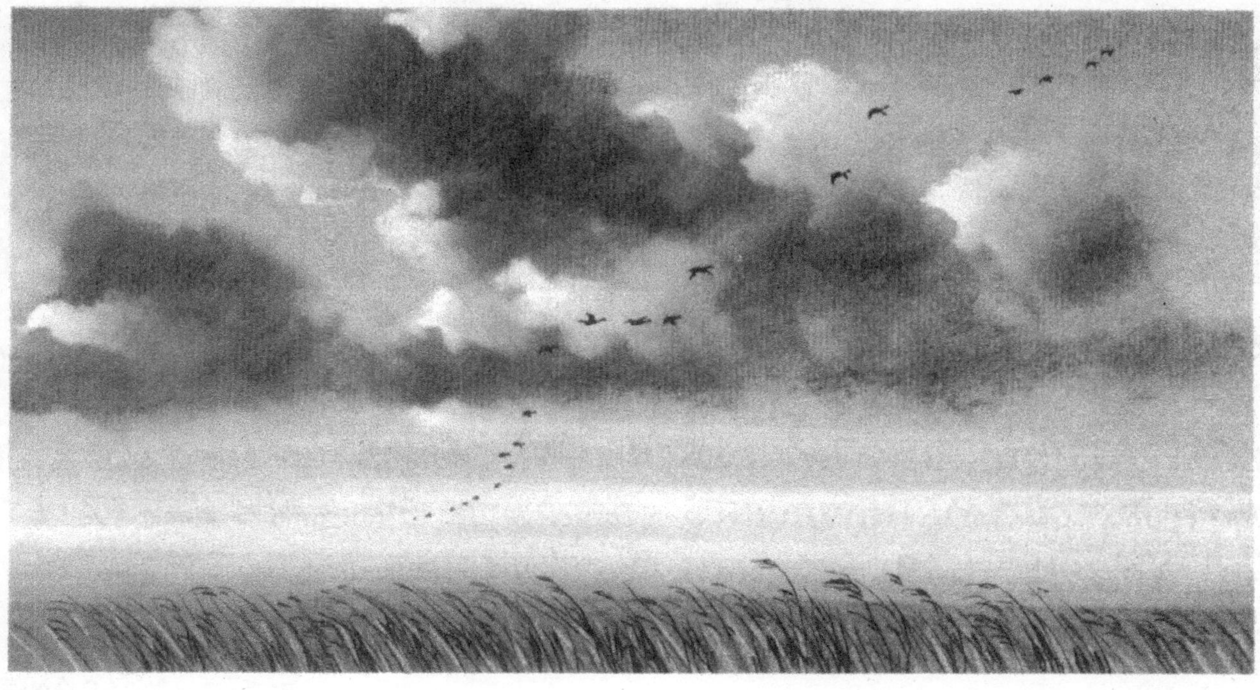

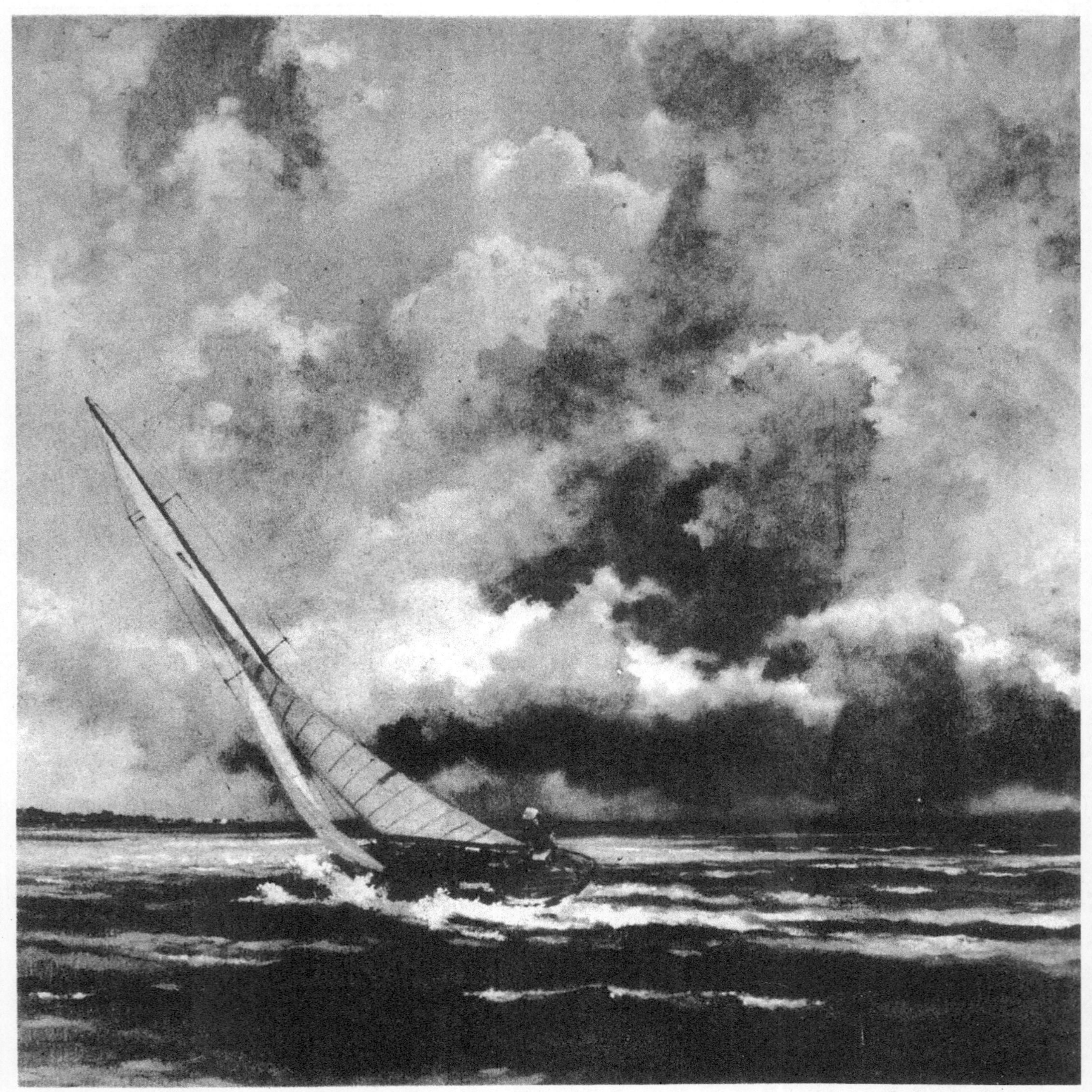

HERE IS A MARINE PAINTING *in* OILS *about* HALF FINISHED. *The* WATER *and* SKY PROGRESS TOGETHER, DEPTH *and* HIGHLIGHTS BEING APPLIED TO BOTH *in* UNISON, SKY *complimenting the* WATER. FROM THIS POINT ON HOWEVER, SEPARATE BRUSHES *and* PALETTES MIGHT WELL BE USED *because the* FINISHING TOUCHES TO THE SKY MUST BE CLEAR, BRILLIANT, UNMUDDIED

ERIC SLOANE
WEATHER HILL, ROSLYN L.I.N.Y.

A CATALOG OF SELECTED

DOVER BOOKS

IN ALL FIELDS OF INTEREST

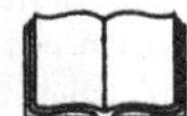

A CATALOG OF SELECTED DOVER BOOKS IN ALL FIELDS OF INTEREST

STICKLEY CRAFTSMAN FURNITURE CATALOGS, Gustav Stickley and L. & J. G. Stickley. Beautiful, functional furniture in two authentic catalogs from 1910. 594 illustrations, including 277 photos, show settles, rockers, armchairs, reclining chairs, bookcases, desks, tables. 183pp. 6½ x 9¼. 0-486-23838-5

AMERICAN LOCOMOTIVES IN HISTORIC PHOTOGRAPHS: 1858 to 1949, Ron Ziel (ed.). A rare collection of 126 meticulously detailed official photographs, called "builder portraits," of American locomotives that majestically chronicle the rise of steam locomotive power in America. Introduction. Detailed captions. xi+129pp. 9 x 12. 0-486-27393-8

AMERICA'S LIGHTHOUSES: An Illustrated History, Francis Ross Holland, Jr. Delightfully written, profusely illustrated fact-filled survey of over 200 American lighthouses since 1716. History, anecdotes, technological advances, more. 240pp. 8 x 10¾. 0-486-25576-X

TOWARDS A NEW ARCHITECTURE, Le Corbusier. Pioneering manifesto by founder of "International School." Technical and aesthetic theories, views of industry, economics, relation of form to function, "mass-production split" and much more. Profusely illustrated. 320pp. 6⅛ x 9¼. (Available in U.S. only.) 0-486-25023-7

HOW THE OTHER HALF LIVES, Jacob Riis. Famous journalistic record, exposing poverty and degradation of New York slums around 1900, by major social reformer. 100 striking and influential photographs. 233pp. 10 x 7⅞. 0-486-22012-5

FRUIT KEY AND TWIG KEY TO TREES AND SHRUBS, William M. Harlow. One of the handiest and most widely used identification aids. Fruit key covers 120 deciduous and evergreen species; twig key 160 deciduous species. Easily used. Over 300 photographs. 126pp. 5⅜ x 8½. 0-486-20511-8

COMMON BIRD SONGS, Dr. Donald J. Borror. Songs of 60 most common U.S. birds: robins, sparrows, cardinals, bluejays, finches, more–arranged in order of increasing complexity. Up to 9 variations of songs of each species.
Cassette and manual 0-486-99911-4

ORCHIDS AS HOUSE PLANTS, Rebecca Tyson Northen. Grow cattleyas and many other kinds of orchids–in a window, in a case, or under artificial light. 63 illustrations. 148pp. 5⅜ x 8½. 0-486-23261-1

MONSTER MAZES, Dave Phillips. Masterful mazes at four levels of difficulty. Avoid deadly perils and evil creatures to find magical treasures. Solutions for all 32 exciting illustrated puzzles. 48pp. 8¼ x 11. 0-486-26005-4

MOZART'S DON GIOVANNI (DOVER OPERA LIBRETTO SERIES), Wolfgang Amadeus Mozart. Introduced and translated by Ellen H. Bleiler. Standard Italian libretto, with complete English translation. Convenient and thoroughly portable–an ideal companion for reading along with a recording or the performance itself. Introduction. List of characters. Plot summary. 121pp. 5¼ x 8½. 0-486-24944-1

FRANK LLOYD WRIGHT'S DANA HOUSE, Donald Hoffmann. Pictorial essay of residential masterpiece with over 160 interior and exterior photos, plans, elevations, sketches and studies. 128pp. 9¼ x 10¾. 0-486-29120-0

LIGHT AND SHADE: A Classic Approach to Three-Dimensional Drawing, Mrs. Mary P. Merrifield. Handy reference clearly demonstrates principles of light and shade by revealing effects of common daylight, sunshine, and candle or artificial light on geometrical solids. 13 plates. 64pp. 5⅜ x 8½. 0-486-44143-1

ASTROLOGY AND ASTRONOMY: A Pictorial Archive of Signs and Symbols, Ernst and Johanna Lehner. Treasure trove of stories, lore, and myth, accompanied by more than 300 rare illustrations of planets, the Milky Way, signs of the zodiac, comets, meteors, and other astronomical phenomena. 192pp. 8⅜ x 11. 0-486-43981-X

JEWELRY MAKING: Techniques for Metal, Tim McCreight. Easy-to-follow instructions and carefully executed illustrations describe tools and techniques, use of gems and enamels, wire inlay, casting, and other topics. 72 line illustrations and diagrams. 176pp. 8¼ x 10⅞. 0-486-44043-5

MAKING BIRDHOUSES: Easy and Advanced Projects, Gladstone Califf. Easy-to-follow instructions include diagrams for everything from a one-room house for bluebirds to a forty-two-room structure for purple martins. 56 plates; 4 figures. 80pp. 8¾ x 6⅜. 0-486-44183-0

LITTLE BOOK OF LOG CABINS: How to Build and Furnish Them, William S. Wicks. Handy how-to manual, with instructions and illustrations for building cabins in the Adirondack style, fireplaces, stairways, furniture, beamed ceilings, and more. 102 line drawings. 96pp. 8¾ x 6⅜. 0-486-44259-4

THE SEASONS OF AMERICA PAST, Eric Sloane. From "sugaring time" and strawberry picking to Indian summer and fall harvest, a whole year's activities described in charming prose and enhanced with 79 of the author's own illustrations. 160pp. 8¼ x 11. 0-486-44220-9

THE METROPOLIS OF TOMORROW, Hugh Ferriss. Generous, prophetic vision of the metropolis of the future, as perceived in 1929. Powerful illustrations of towering structures, wide avenues, and rooftop parks–all features in many of today's modern cities. 59 illustrations. 144pp. 8¼ x 11. 0-486-43727-2

THE PATH TO ROME, Hilaire Belloc. This 1902 memoir abounds in lively vignettes from a vanished time, recounting a pilgrimage on foot across the Alps and Apennines in order to "see all Europe which the Christian Faith has saved." 77 of the author's original line drawings complement his sparkling prose. 272pp. 5⅜ x 8½. 0-486-44001-X

THE HISTORY OF RASSELAS: Prince of Abissinia, Samuel Johnson. Distinguished English writer attacks eighteenth-century optimism and man's unrealistic estimates of what life has to offer. 112pp. 5⅜ x 8½. 0-486-44094-X

A VOYAGE TO ARCTURUS, David Lindsay. A brilliant flight of pure fancy, where wild creatures crowd the fantastic landscape and demented torturers dominate victims with their bizarre mental powers. 272pp. 5⅜ x 8½. 0-486-44198-9

Paperbound unless otherwise indicated. Available at your book dealer, online at **www.doverpublications.com**, or by writing to Dept. GI, Dover Publications, Inc., 31 East 2nd Street, Mineola, NY 11501. For current price information or for free catalogs (please indicate field of interest), write to Dover Publications or log on to **www.doverpublications.com** and see every Dover book in print. Dover publishes more than 500 books each year on science, elementary and advanced mathematics, biology, music, art, literary history, social sciences, and other areas.